TS
156.6
.P87
1992

ISO
CERTIFICATION

●

TOTAL QUALITY
MANAGEMENT

ISO 9000
CERTIFICATION
and
TOTAL QUALITY
MANAGEMENT

281207487

Subhash C. Puri

Standards-Quality Management Group
Ottawa and Washington, D.C.

Canadian Cataloguing in Publication Data

Puri, Subhash C.
ISO 9000 certification and total quality management

Includes bibliographical references and index.
ISBN 0-9695927-0-1

1. Quality control--Standards. 2. Total quality management.
I. Standards-Quality Management Group. II. Title.

TS156.6.P87 1992   658.5'62   C92-090145-X

ISBN   0-9695927-0-1

Standards-Quality Management Group

P.O. Box 66654
Washington Square
Washington, D.C. 20035
U.S.A.

P.O. Box 4146, Station "C"
Ottawa, Ontario K1Y 4P2
Canada
Tel./Fax: (613) 820-2445

Dedication

To my wife: **Shashi**
and daughters: **Pamela and Anuradha**
for their patience, understanding and support

CONTENTS

PART TWO: ISO 9000 CERTIFICATION

FOREWORD

From my visits throughout the world in recent years, I can say categorically that amongst business, government, producers and consumers there is unprecedented interest world-wide in superior levels of quality for goods and services. There is rapidly increasing recognition that managing for optimum quality is not only desirable but also imperative. It means for the producer better profitability with increased productivity, lower costs, less waste, enhanced competitiveness; for the consumer, greater satisfaction and better value; for governments, an essential element in strengthening the economies of their countries. I attribute the drive for quality improvement to several factors:

- the lowering and removing of barriers to trade between nations, and hence a more competitive world,
- management realization in recent years about providing the kind of leadership necessary for higher levels of quality performance,
- the development of new tools to help achieve quality performance,
- minimizing the cost-burden of carrying inventory through quality performance.

To provide organizations - industrial, commercial or government - with quality system standards and guidelines, the International Organization for Standardization developed the ISO 9000 series of international standards. Published in 1987, these standards are sweeping the world and should be used without change, without additions or deletions.

In his book "ISO 9000 Certification and Total Quality Management", Subhash Puri lays out easy-to-follow, step-by-step procedures for implementing quality systems and for fulfilling external quality assurance requirements by qualifying for registration to the appropriate ISO 9000 standard.

The author has earned an enviable reputation for his contributions to the appreciation and understanding of quality management and quality assurance through several books and professional papers over the last two decades. This new publication is a valuable addition to the series and the author should be congratulated for his comprehensive and timely book on the subject.

Roy A. Phillips, CM. B.A.Sc., P.Eng.
ISO President (1989-91)

xi

PREFACE

"The quality revolution continues..."

Pursuit for quality and excellence is not new. We have always wanted good quality products and services, and we always will. This desire for quality is ingrained in us. In the past, there were relatively fewer producers and the products were limited in variety, volume and innovativeness. Consequently, compromises were necessary at the altar of quality in order to obtain the right product at the right price. Today, world markets are intensely competitive and abound in product variety, volume, complexity and innovativeness. As a result, it is now relatively easier for buyers and consumers to expect, demand and receive quality products and services at competitive prices.

In this market-driven environment, marketability and, therefore, profitability is dependent on quality, competitive pricing, and customer satisfaction. Quality improvement comes through developing, implementing and maintaining a Total Quality Management (TQM) System. A TQM System comprises all aspects of management, systems, procedures, processes and methodologies properly coordinated, with an absolute focus on customer satisfaction. In addition, quality improvement requires management commitment, constancy of purpose, employee empowerment and a supplier-customer partnering.

Having implemented an effective quality system and achieved a certain level of quality, an enterprise would often like to seek a seal of approval and accreditation to the achieved quality status. The quality system accreditation is generally carried out by a third-party accredited organization, known as the Registrar, against an established and universally accepted standard. To fill this gap, the International Organization for Standardization (ISO), through its technical committee "ISO/TC 176: Quality Management and Quality Assurance", has developed a three-tier set of generic quality system standards, the ISO-9000 series. These standards can be used for several purposes: as guidelines to establish a quality system, as two-party contractual documents between the buyer and the seller to assure a stipulated quality level, and as a protocol for third-party accreditation and certification. Since its inception in 1987, the ISO-9000 series of Quality System Standards has been adopted by most industrialized nations, either as their national standards or along with and parallel to their national standards.

There is a standards-driven quality revolution and the market forces are directing companies to seek third-party evidence based on conformance to one of the levels in the ISO-9000 series. Conformance to the international quality standards is becoming a business mandate of the 1990's. Despite the fact that there is a consequent rush by companies to implement quality systems and seek ISO-9000 certification, there is, unfortunately, little assistance available on how to proceed and prepare for registration. This book attempts to fill that gap. Since the establishment of an effective total quality system is almost a prerequisite to achieving ISO-9000 certification, the book begins by describing the most important and most popular approaches for developing and implementing a TQM System. It then deals with the subject of ISO-9000 certification and provides a very comprehensive set of guidelines with an action checklist for registration to any of the ISO-9000 standards.

The author wishes to thank Tammy Chamberlain for her devoted assistance in the preparation of this book, to Roger Trudel for his excellent professional and editorial comments, to Suraj Harish for his expert design work and to Dr. Vince DiTullio, James Fulford and Patricia Kopp for their continued support and inspiration. I also wish to thank all the authors and associations who gave their permission to use excerpts and references from their publications. Lastly, I wish to express my profound gratitude to my wife Shashi and my two daughters Pamela and Anuradha for their patience and support throughout this project.

Ottawa, Canada   **Subhash C. Puri**

ONE

THE QUALITY IMPERATIVE

◆ QUALITY-PRODUCTIVITY ERA

Within the industrialized infrastructure of at least the developed countries, the 90's constitute what is being called a Quality-Productivity Era. Quality seems to be the single most profoundly sought and aggressively pursued entity in the manufacturing as well as in the service world today.

Product quality was really not a big issue a few decades ago, because the only producers of finished products were a few industrialized countries and whatever they produced was either consumed and utilized internally or could be conveniently sold to the majority of non-producing, developing countries.

The global order has changed considerably. The world market of today is steadily shrinking and is becoming intensely competitive. There are many more producers than ever before. With the rapid growth of scientific knowledge and advanced technology, the newly emerging producers, being labour-intensive, are able to compete favourably with the highly industrialized capital-intensive producers. In some cases, they are even capable of surpassing them in terms of volume, variety and low-cost production, if not in quality.

There is almost a universal concordance that the most essential factors for survival and growth, for an enterprise in a highly competitive environment such as this, are: high quality, increased productivity, cost-effectiveness and customer satisfaction. Quality is the key to pride, productivity and profitability. It is the basic entity that differentiates between an excellent company and a mediocre company.

1

◆ MARKET-DRIVEN QUALITY

Pursuit for quality is virtually market-driven. Changes in the environment exert enormous influences on the nature and extent of market operability. It is, therefore, imperative that the strategic planning framework for improving quality be commensurate with the market environment. What are the key factors influencing today's environment? Let us look at these in terms of five elements: the markets, products, producer, consumer, and regulatory/standards agency.

Markets

- It is a highly entrepreneurial, highly competitive world market today.
- Quality volatility is high due to the differential between labour-intensiveness and capital-intensiveness.
- Markets are dichotomously indecisive - attempting to diminish trade barriers while still upholding the protectionistic stance.
- Quality, competitive pricing and constancy of purpose holds the key to marketability.

Products

- Products are continuously increasing in complexity, variety and volume.
- Market-driven pressures on product lines include: high quality, innovativeness, economic competitiveness and affordability, conformance to regulatory and other requirements, safety and reliability.

Producer

- Producers are under continuous pressure to cope with the multiplicity of product lines, complexity and variety of products, regulatory requirements, and consumer expectations.
- There is a constant struggle for profitability, credibility and continued market share.
- Financial constraints and human resources volatility are high.

Consumer

- Consumer awareness for quality, safety, and competitive pricing is very high.
- Consumers are increasingly demanding variety, innovativeness, product dependability, better post-sales service and warranties.

Regulatory/Standards Agency

- Greater emphasis is being placed on standardized procedures and processes, consumer protection, cost-effectiveness, safety, enforcement of regulations, cost-recovery, privatization, and deregulation.

◆ THE ENTERPRISE MISSION

In all this market-driven quality scenario, every enterprise, large or small, manufacturing or service, has some fundamental reason/motive for existence. The four key driving forces are:

- Profitability
- Expanded market share
- Long-term survival
- Service to society

The continued realization of these goals is highly dependent on an enterprise's ability and determination to:

- Improve quality and productivity.
- Reduce costs.
- Meet product/service/regulatory/standards requirements.
- Achieve complete customer confidence/satisfaction/delight.
- Improve reputation and credibility.
- Improve market share.
- Remain competitive.

The strategic focus for improving quality, profitability and competitive position requires:

- Total management commitment
- Development of a quality culture
- Constancy of purpose
- Consistency in superior quality output
- Effective employee participation and empowerment
- Partnering with suppliers and customers
- Development and implementation of effective quality systems
- Development of a mission, vision and continuous improvement strategy

◆ QUALITY CONCERNS

Why do we want quality? Quality is the basic entity that differentiates between a mediocre and an excellent company. It is absolutely fundamental to marketability, profitability and survival. Following are some of the intrinsic and extrinsic gains that can be realized through improved quality:

Intrinsic Gains

- Reduced costs
- Reduced scrap/waste
- Improved control of operations
- Improved predictability and reliability
- Increased efficiency/productivity
- Increased compliance
- Improved confidence, pride and profitability

Extrinsic Gains

- Improved competitiveness and marketability
- Expanded and continued market share
- Improved credibility, reputation and dependability
- Ability/capability to balance out the differential between labour-intensiveness and capital-intensiveness
- Customer satisfaction/delight
- Service to society

Every enterprise has at least two fundamental concerns about quality:

- How to achieve quality? What methods/means should be used to implement, maintain and continuously improve quality?
- Having achieved quality, how to demonstrate the achievement? How to get accreditation and recognition of the achievement? How to let everyone know that this company is operating and committed to the highest levels of quality?

Quality improvement concerns are addressed by developing, implementing and maintaining a Total Quality Management System. To implement a TQM System, a company can either develop its own program based on the fundamental principles of quality, or can use the approach outlined in ISO-9004, or can follow philosophies and methodologies propounded by the famous quality experts and gurus such as: Deming, Juran, Crosby, Feigenbaum, Ishikawa, etc.

Demonstration of the fact that a company has actually achieved a certain level of quality can be done either by the process of accreditation and certification to the ISO-9000 series of international quality system standards or by achieving the acceptability criteria of one of the existing quality prizes and awards such as: the Malcolm Baldrige Award, the Deming Prize, NASA's Quality and Excellence Award, the Canada Award for Business Excellence, etc.

◆ TOWARDS A DEFINITION OF QUALITY

Before proceeding any further, it would be in order to first understand the meaning of the word "quality". The word "quality" is much like the word "stress" - a profoundly fashionable term that has become an integral part of the popular lexicon. Yet, it has as many meanings and interpretations as there are people who experience it.

Quality is indeed a complex and multifaceted concept. It is not a singular activity or characteristic, nor a system or department. It is the sum total of all characteristics of a product or service that contributes to its superiority and excellence.

Quality has been defined in a variety of ways. Table 1 lists some of the popularly used definitions of "quality", including the one developed by the International Organization for Standardization (ISO), in the international standard: "ISO-8402: Quality Vocabulary". ISO-8402 and its subsequent addendum currently under preparation, ISO-8402-1, also contain several other quality related definitions.

◆ TOTAL QUALITY MANAGEMENT

Quality is not a tactical but a strategic issue. Quality does not come through piecemeal efforts or through a single quality improvement program, procedure or process. It is the result of a totally integrated set of actions with a long-term commitment. Quality is not a short-term function but a long-term focus.

Table 1. Quality: Definitions

- Quality is customer satisfaction/delight.
- Quality means conformance to specified requirements.
- Quality means fitness for use.
- Quality means value for money.
- Quality means zero defects.
- Quality means guarantee of confidence.
- Quality is efficiency and productivity.
- Quality is an investment for profitability.
- Quality means on-time delivery.
- Quality is a collective attitude of mind.
- Quality is thought revolution in management.
- Quality means innate excellence.
- Quality is a systematic approach to excellence.
- Quality is the ultimate expression of craftsmanship.
- Quality is excellence in output.
- Quality is a never-ending cycle of improvement.
- Quality means constancy of purpose.
- Quality means pride of ownership.
- Quality means consistently producing conforming product.
- Quality means credibility.
- Quality means continued and expanded market share.
- Quality means loss imparted to society from the time a product is shipped (Japanese).

ISO-8402 (1986): Quality Vocabulary

- Quality is the totality of features and characteristics of a product or service that bears on its ability to satisfy stated or implied needs.

- Quality is all of the above.

Quality cannot be instantly manufactured; it is infused and embedded into a product through systematic means. Quality is achieved, piece by piece, process by process, within the overall umbrella of a total quality management system. It must be clearly understood that today when we talk of quality, we mean the quality of all aspects of production such as: the quality of products and services, the quality of work-life, employee involvement and empowerment, productivity improvement, competitive position, customer satisfaction, etc. A total quality system encompasses all the processes that collectively contribute to the achievement of total quality.

Total quality systems are referenced through several different names: TQM (Total Quality Management), TQA (Total Quality Assurance), CWQC (Company-Wide Quality Control, used by the Japanese), TQC (Total Quality Control), TQI (Total Quality Improvement), CQA (Corporate Quality Assurance), SQM (Strategic Quality Management), etc.

Total Quality Management (TQM) can, perhaps, be defined as follows:

- TQM refers to the totality of functions necessary for the overall management of products and services to achieve the highest levels of quality.
- TQM involves the application of quantitative methods and human resources to improve the material and services supplied to an organization.
- TQM integrates philosophy, customer focus, guiding principles, fundamental management techniques, and technical tools and systems to provide a disciplined approach to continuous improvement.

The definition of TQM given in the committee draft of the International Standard, "ISO/CD 8402-1: Quality Concepts and Terminology - Part 1: Generic Terms and Definitions", is as follows:

> **"Total Quality Management**: A management approach of an organization, centered on quality, based on the participation of all its members and aiming at long-term profitability through customer satisfaction, including benefits to the members of the organization and to society."

Some other important quality related definitions included in ISO/CD 8402-1 are appended below for reference.

"**Quality Management**: All activities of the overall management function that determine the quality policy, objectives and responsibilities and implement them by means such as quality planning, quality control, quality assurance and quality improvement."

"**Quality Control**: The operational techniques and activities that are used to fulfil requirements for quality."

"**Quality Assurance**: All the planned and systematic actions to be implemented, and demonstrated as needed, necessary to provide adequate confidence that an entity will satisfy given requirements for quality."

"**Quality Planning**: Establishing and developing the objectives and requirements for quality and the requirements for the quality system application."

"**Quality System**: The organizational structure, responsibilities, procedures, processes and resources for implementing quality management."

"**Quality Improvement**: The actions taken to increase the value to the customer by improving the effectiveness and efficiency of processes and activities throughout the quality loop."

Before proceeding further, a clear understanding of the distinction between the traditional and modern approaches to quality improvement is imperative. As market competitiveness increases, so does the demand for quality and excellence. Different companies react differently to this demand. Some companies keep their focus limited to only the quality of products and after-sales services. Consequently, their efforts are centered around the traditional approaches to quality, ie., quality control, process control and quality assurance of the final product. Then, there are other companies who are committed to a long-term quality focus. Their concern is much broader than merely the quality of products and services. Their preoccupation is with the quality of all aspects of work-life, ie., quality of work environment, employee involvement, empowerment and pride of workmanship, quality of products and services, productivity improvement, total customer satisfaction, market credibility and reputation, expanded market share, etc. The emphasis, therefore, is on establishing a TQM System with a strong focus on continuous improvement.

Sustained quality excellence requires constancy of purpose and commitment. The long-term quality focus is achieved through the establishment and maintenance of a TQM System. Although process improvement is fundamentally an essential part of quality improvement, today's competitive environment makes it mandatory to think in terms of total quality management. A TQM System encompasses all aspects of management, systems, procedures, processes and methodologies put together in a coordinated and correlational whole. Thus, even when most companies are genuinely interested in improving quality, the lack of understanding between implementing a TQM System and attempting to merely improve the processes ultimately leads to unfulfilled expectations, failures and frustrations.

◆ BEYOND THE HORIZON

While quality and quality system certification is imperative, there is something more fundamentally important beyond the horizon that all proactive organizations must sensitize themselves to - "the competitive survivability". At the moment, our preoccupation is with establishing total quality systems and achieving recognition through certification to international quality assurance standards, such as the ISO-9000 series. This is important as well as imperative. It would help companies achieve a competitive edge against both the labour-intensive markets and the capital-intensive markets. However, crystal-balling is essential for strategic planning for those futuristic situations when most companies would have achieved higher quality status. Then, the competition would be intensely fierce and survival would require additional strategic action. The most fundamental such action that would help keep companies afloat is to produce more, more cheaply and consistently better.

Excellent companies are those who would not wait to take necessary steps before they are thrown into the competitive pit; they would plan now and ensure that the proper action is integrated and implemented with their operational planning framework and infrastructure. Essentially, companies have to be cognizant of and work towards the following:

- Establish self-correcting and self-rejuvenating quality systems.
- Keep strong emphasis on continuous quality maintenance and improvement.
- Improve productivity and reduce costs.
- Provide competitive pricing.
- Establish long-term partnership with customers.

It must, therefore, be clearly understood that although quality is fundamentally important, it is not the only ingredient in the formula for success. Quality has to be accompanied by constancy of purpose, high productivity, competitive pricing and customer satisfaction.

◆ BOOK LAYOUT

In response to the quality concerns identified above, this book is divided into two parts and addresses in full detail the following aspects of quality:

- Part I: Development and Implementation of a TQM System
- Part II: Preparation for ISO-9000 Registration/Certification

Part I outlines the various approaches in establishing a TQM System and provides a complete road map for developing, implementing and maintaining a total quality management and improvement system. Also included is a brief description of the various quality system accreditation programs, awards and prizes currently available.

Part II is exclusively devoted to the preparation and achievement of certification status to the ISO-9000 Quality System Standards. It provides a complete and detailed set of guidelines to assist in the effective interpretation of quality system elements, methods of developing quality system documentation, and procedures of quality system auditing; it is further accompanied by a detailed action checklist.

PART ONE

TOTAL QUALITY

MANAGEMENT

TWO

DEVELOPING A TQM MODEL

◆ INTRODUCTION

As indicated earlier, different organizations react differently to quality improvement pressures. Those in the reactive mode have generally a short-term focus and, consequently, their efforts are limited to quality control and quality assurance activities to improve the quality of their products and services. Proactive organizations operate on long-term goals. Their efforts are expended on improving the quality of all aspects of work-life. While ensuring continuous quality improvement of their products and services, these companies are also concerned about the welfare of their employees, total customer satisfaction, partnership with their suppliers/subcontractors, and service to society in general. By doing so, they virtually guarantee for themselves an expanded marketability, continuous growth, high productivity, profitability and long-term survivability.

Quality concerns, short-term as well as long-term, are effectively addressed by establishing a Total Quality Management (TQM) System. A TQM System can be developed and established through a variety of ways. For instance, a company can develop its own TQM System based on the fundamental principles of quality or choose to follow the approach outlined in ISO-9004 or yet follow the philosophies and methodologies propounded by various quality experts and gurus. The following approaches to TQM are discussed in Part One of this book:

- Self-Developed/Self-Directed TQM System
- TQM Model via ISO-9004
- TQM Model: Additional Approaches (Deming, Juran, Crosby)
- TQM Model: Service Industries

◆ SELF-DEVELOPED/SELF-DIRECTED TQM SYSTEM

Typically, a TQM System, irrespective of any approach or philosophy, would have at least the following components:

- Quality philosophy and management responsibilities
- Quality policies, plans, systems, procedures and processes
- Quality tools and methodologies

Some of the essential elements in these three components of a TQM system would include the following:

Management Responsibilities

- Vision
- Mission
- Commitment
- Responsibility
- Cultural Change
- Leadership

- Employee Involvement
- Teamwork
- Support Systems
- Disciplined Methodology
- Knowledge and Skills
- Customer Focus

Support Systems

- Procurement Control
- Design Control
- Production Control
- Process Control
- Inspection/Testing
- Nonconformity
- Corrective Action
- Cost Control
- Documentation

- Evaluation
- Quality Audits
- Verification Control
- Quality Records
- Training
- Servicing
- Marketing Control
- Post-Production Control
- Customer Feedback

Tools and Methodologies

- Brainstorming
- Flow Chart
- Checksheet
- Histogram
- Cause-Effect Diagram
- Pareto Chart
- Trend Chart
- Scatter Diagram

- Quality Function Deployment (QFD)
- Force Field Analysis
- Shewhart - Deming Cycle
- Nominal Group Technique
- Benchmarking
- Block Diagram
- Relations Diagram

- Control Charts
- Statistical Process Control (SPC)
- Design of Experiments
- Systematic/Tree Diagram
- Arrow Diagram

- Affinity Diagram/KJ Method
- Matrix Diagram
- Matrix Data - Analysis
- Process Decision Program Chart (PDPC)
- Concurrent Engineering

In order to develop a customized TQM model from the system elements listed above, the company first needs to clarify and delineate an overall road map by identifying the requisite elements appropriate to each of the following components:

- The Mission
- The Vision
- The Customer
- The Supplier
- The Company

The Mission

- Clearly define the company's business.
- Identify the company's needs, interests and mission.
- Who are the current customers?
- Who are the potential customers?
- Identify the customer requirements.
- Assess the company's current capabilities vis-à-vis the customer requirements.
- Identify the company's strengths and weaknesses.
- Determine what needs to be done to meet the customer's needs and expectations.
- Identify the changes, modifications, or improvements required in the company's operations to accomplish the mission.
- Determine the company's competitors as well as their strengths and weaknesses.
- Identify how and by what means the company can gain a competitive edge.

The Vision

- For long-term strategic planning, establish the company's vision.
- Develop long-term goals and objectives.
- Identify the potential customers and their requirements.
- Identify how the company's capabilities need to be realigned or augmented to meet the requirements of the potential customers.

- Who are likely to be the company's potential competitors? Identify their strengths and weaknesses.
- Plan, strategize and act to gain a competitive edge.

The Customer

- Customer satisfaction is the primary goal. Establish a long-term relationship with the customer and identify how this will be achieved.
- Identify the customer's total needs and expectations.
- Establish the infrastructure necessary for continuous dialogue with the customer to clearly understand his requirements.
- Translate the customer's needs into operational actions.

The Supplier

- Identify the materials, supplies, equipment and subcontracted tasks needed to provide products and services as per the customer's requirements.
- Select appropriate suppliers and subcontractors.
- Establish a partnership with your suppliers to ensure a continuous supply of high quality materials.
- Liaise with the suppliers and establish suitable materiel control procedures.
- Establish effective communication with the suppliers to clarify your requirements.
- Develop an appropriate materiel verification system.

The Company

- Plan and generate a global framework for a total quality management system commensurate with the strategic requirements identified in the mission, vision, and customer/supplier interface.
- Establish the quality policy and objectives.
- Identify management commitment.
- Define and establish the quality infrastructure and responsibilities.
- Develop quality plans and appropriate systems.
- Identify quality procedures, processes and methodologies.
- Implement quality improvement projects and initiatives.
- Involve everyone in the company through process improvement teams.
- Implement process improvement strategies.
- Establish a quality audit/verification system.
- Measure, analyze and assess performance.
- Institute an effective corrective/preventive action mechanism.
- Establish a continuous cycle of improvement.
- Maintain focus on customer satisfaction.

Once a complete road map has been outlined, the basic framework of a TQM System can be easily established. The system has to be well structured and documented so that everyone in the company can follow it consistently and uniformly. A typical TQM program would have the following basic elements:

- **Management:** vision, mission, commitment, leadership, quality policy and objectives

- **Strategic Planning:** quality plans, procedures, processes, activities; quality infrastructure

- **Human Resource Management:** employee involvement and empowerment, process improvement teams, education and training

- **Input Controls:** market analysis, customer needs, incoming quality assurance, supplier-customer partnering

- **In-Process Controls:** control of design, specifications, material, equipment; process control; documentation control; production control; process/product audit and verification

- **Measurement / Analysis:** data collection and analysis, statistical process control (SPC)

- **Output Controls:** output audit and verification, conformance to contractual and regulatory requirements

- **Customer Satisfaction:** customer requirements and expectations, service standards, commitment, complaint resolution, satisfaction determination, satisfaction results

◆ THE 7-STEP TQM MODEL

From the above discussion, we can now draw up a workable TQM model as schematically illustrated in Table 2. To implement the system, the company must develop a corporate TQM guidebook describing, step-by-step, all its operational functions, procedures, and processes, commensurate with the model. The following describe the major areas of consideration to be included in this documentation:

Step 1: Management

- Develop a mission statement.
- Identify the company's vision.
- Identify management commitment and a long-term perspective.

- Involve people in the quality process through a steering committee and process improvement teams.
- Identify the process by which customer needs and expectations are communicated, understood and fulfilled.
- Specify the cross-functional support systems utilized for the quality system.
- Identify the precise and structured methods, procedures and techniques used to improve quality.
- Delineate how education and training needs are met.

Step 2: Mission

- First determine the customer's needs and requirements.
- Next identify the company's mission with respect to the suppliers and subcontractors.
- Finally define and establish the company's own infrastructure, responsibilities and requirements needed to interface with the suppliers and to satisfy the customer.

Step 3: Processes

- Identify all the processes impacting quality.
- Describe all process requirements.
- Establish improvement goals and priorities.

Step 4: Projects

- Establish and implement improvement projects.
- Develop a measurement system to assess performance.

Step 5: Continuous Improvement

- Collect data to analyze the processes and projects.
- Institute appropriate corrective/preventive measures.
- Identify improvement opportunities.
- Develop strategic initiatives.
- Implement additional improvement projects.

Step 6: Evaluation

- Establish audit/evaluation procedures.
- Identify the system's strengths and weaknesses.
- Take appropriate management decisions.

Step 7: Review/Revision

- Repeat the continuous improvement cycle.

Table 2. The 7-Step TQM Model

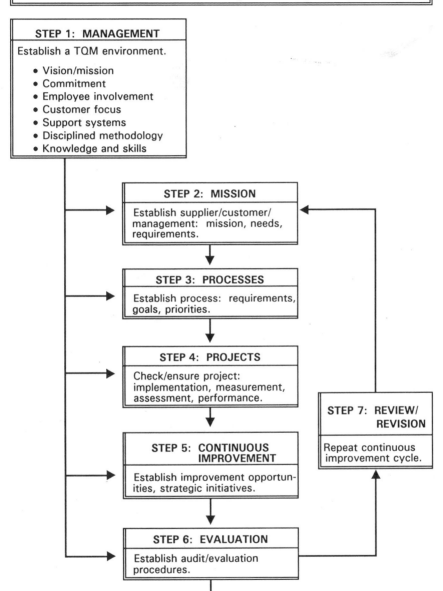

STEP 1: MANAGEMENT

Establish a TQM environment.

- Vision/mission
- Commitment
- Employee involvement
- Customer focus
- Support systems
- Disciplined methodology
- Knowledge and skills

STEP 2: MISSION

Establish supplier/customer/ management: mission, needs, requirements.

STEP 3: PROCESSES

Establish process: requirements, goals, priorities.

STEP 4: PROJECTS

Check/ensure project: implementation, measurement, assessment, performance.

STEP 7: REVIEW/ REVISION

Repeat continuous improvement cycle.

STEP 5: CONTINUOUS IMPROVEMENT

Establish improvement opportunities, strategic initiatives.

STEP 6: EVALUATION

Establish audit/evaluation procedures.

QUALITY LAND

◆ TQM IMPLEMENTATION PLAN

Consider the following systematic sequence of steps for the implementation of the 7-Step TQM model outlined in Table 2.

Phase One

- Ensure management commitment.
- Foster management awareness/education/discussion.
- Establish a TQM Steering Committee.
- Appoint a TQM coordinator.
- Develop a TQM mission statement.
- Identify/document a quality policy.
- Develop quality objectives.
- Provide employee orientation/awareness/education.

Phase Two

- Partner with suppliers and identify needs/requirements/mission.
- Partner with customers and identify needs/requirements/mission.
- Develop constancy/trust with suppliers and customers.
- Identify management responsibilities/mission commensurate with supplier - customer partnering.

Phase Three

- Identify all processes in the total production cycle, from the procurement of raw material to the supply of finished product.
- Create Process Improvement Teams (PIT's).
- Define process boundaries and requirements for each process.
- Define the current best process.
- Establish goals and priorities.
- Identify process control/improvement requirements and requisite resources.

Phase Four

- Implement control/improvement projects.
- Establish measures of performance.
- Assess conformance to specified requirements.
- Eliminate process variability - control processes.
- Bring process under statistical control.
- Assess process capability.
- Take corrective/preventive action.

Phase Five

- Identify improvement opportunities.
- Establish strategic initiatives.
- Identify/allocate requisite resources.
- Continue process improvement.

Phase Six

- Establish audit/evaluation procedures.
- Review each process and take corrective/preventive action.

Phase Seven

- Repeat the entire cycle of activities, initiatives and actions to continuously improve the system.

◆ PROCESS IMPROVEMENT PLAN

The overall quality system is generally a sum total of many processes. To improve the overall system, therefore, it is imperative to concentrate efforts on improving the processes. Some of the key considerations for process improvement involve the following:

- Identify all the processes that impact quality.
- Define the current capability of the process.
- Specify the expected/required capability.
- Identify and implement improvement initiatives.
- Bring the process under statistical control.
- Analyze the process.
- Measure its performance and assess its process capability.
- Identify improvement actions and strategies.
- Repeat the continuous improvement cycle.

Consider the following four-step plan for process improvement:

Step One

- Select/define the process of interest.
- Organize PIT's (Process Improvement Teams).
- Define process boundaries/requirements.
- Establish process flow charts.
- Assess/define the present status of the process.

Step Two

- Define the process output quality.
- Identify the supplier/customer capabilities, requirements and mission.
- List the key quality characteristics.
- Set goals/priorities on the quality characteristics.

Step Three

- Identify/establish a process measurement system for the key quality characteristics.
- Obtain data/information on the process operations.
- Analyze the data with statistical process control methods.
- Identify/eliminate the causes of variability.
- Bring the process under statistical control.
- Assess the process capability.

Step Four

- Adjust the process to aim.
- Identify the key process variables.
- Evaluate cause-effect relationships for the process characteristics and the process variables.
- Reduce/eliminate variability in the process variables and consequently in the process characteristics.
- Identify improvement initiatives.
- Innovate and continuously improve the process.

◆ TQM: THE PRODUCT PROFILE

Consider now an overall application of the TQM system elements defined in the preceding sections, as they apply to the total product profile. We outline the life cycle of a product and identify its corresponding requisite TQM system elements.

Product

- Customer needs
- Market analysis
- Total product profile
- Profit-cost ratio

Design

- Design qualification, requalification
- Design verification
- Design review/change control
- Market readiness

Procurement

- Qualified suppliers
- Receiving inspection
- Verification methods
- Quality records

Production

- Supplies, utilities, environment
- Production control
- Process control
- Process capability

Inspection

- Product identification, disposition
- Documentation
- Problem analysis
- Corrective action
- Preventive action

Marketing

- Handling, packaging and delivery
- Identification and traceability

Servicing

- Warranties, complaints
- Corrective action
- Continued post-sales service

Market Analysis

- Customer satisfaction
- Market changes
- Competition

◆ TEAM APPROACH TO QUALITY

One of the major components of any TQM program is employee involvement and empowerment. Quality does not come through isolated and disjointed efforts; it is the result of the collective effort of all the employees at every level within the organization. As well, leadership plays a significant role in the effective functioning of teams. This section provides some guidelines on the following basic elements:

- Quality leadership
- TQM Steering Committee
- Process Improvement Team (PIT)

Quality Leadership

Total quality management requires a total management transformation. To achieve sustained quality, the traditional roles of supervisors and managers have to be replaced by proactive quality leaders. Table 3 presents some of the fundamental areas where a shift in quality approach is necessary.

Table 3. Management Transformation	
Traditional Managers ⟶	**Proactive Leaders**
• Short-range view	• Long-range perspective
• Focus on mission	• Focus on mission and vision
• Focus on system, structure	• Focus on people
• Controlling people	• Inspiring people
• Administering people	• Innovating people
• Blaming workers	• Sharing responsibility
• Accepting status quo	• Challenging status quo
• Focus on maintenance	• Focus on development
• Focus on fixing, correcting	• Focus on prevention
• Focus on imitation	• Focus on originality
• Doing things right	• Doing right things

Today's quality environment requires dedicated and committed leaders. The success of any TQM System is highly dependent on the people who manage, lead, drive and re-energize the system. Following are some of the typical attributes and deeds displayed by a good leader:

- Focuses on the customer.
- Possesses an absolute clarity of direction, goals, mission and vision.
- Has a complete determination, dedication and commitment to quality and constancy of purpose.
- Continually challenges the processes and works at improving the system.
- Has an obsession with continuous improvement.
- Functions through teamwork and helps to create more leaders.
- Motivates and encourages employees, models the way and inspires a shared vision.
- Provides judgement, direction as well as coaching.
- Listens, forgives and generates trust.
- Understands system/process variability and works towards achieving constancy and predictability.
- Continually improves through training and education.

TQM Steering Committee

At the top of the quality hierarchy pyramid, the Steering Committee comprises the management representatives and the process improvement team leaders. It establishes quality strategies and improvement initiatives and oversees the effective implementation of the total quality management system. Some of the basic roles and functions of the committee are as follows:

- Developing effective quality strategies.
- Identifying and initiating quality improvement projects that have the best chance of success.
- Identifying requisite resources.
- Monitoring progress.
- Addressing/solving problems identified through PIT's and initiating preventive actions.
- Providing guidance and technical assistance.
- Providing leadership.
- Identifying and providing suitable education and training opportunities.
- Maintaining effective communication lines and employee involvement.
- Ensuring a strong customer focus in the TQM System.

Process Improvement Team (PIT)

For each process that collectively contributes to the overall quality system structure, a process improvement team must be established, comprising a team leader and some key personnel responsible for the process quality improvement. A PIT provides a platform for problem identification/resolution, process improvement and employee involvement/empowerment. The basic operational framework of a PIT involves the following components:

- Enhanced communication and involvement
- Exchange of ideas and learning from the opinions of others
- Collection and analysis of meaningful data and information
- Identification of the root causes of problems
- Developing appropriate and optimal solutions
- Planning and implementing suitable changes
- Recommending quality improvement initiatives, opportunities and strategies
- Helping to achieve teamwork and establish a quality culture

◆ TQM: THE FINALE

Summarizing the above discussion on TQM, the following order of events is recommended for the implementation of a TQM System:

- Top management undergoes TQM orientation.
- Top management and senior executives become involved and lead the way.
- Management identifies commitment, makes quality the top priority and establishes a strategic quality plan.
- The company seeks customer involvement and input.
- Employees at all levels are trained in appropriate aspects of TQM.
- Employee involvement is sought through the establishment of a TQM Steering Committee and Process Improvement Teams (PIT's).
- Qualified suppliers are identified and a quality partnership is established.
- Management develops a quality policy and corresponding objectives.
- A cross-functional quality infrastructure is established with an appropriate delineation of responsibilities.
- TQM elements, procedures and processes are developed and adopted on a consistent basis.
- Quality improvement projects and initiatives are implemented.
- Data and information are collected and analyzed to study the effectiveness of the TQM System.

- System deficiencies are corrected and preventive measures are implemented.
- Quality is improved and the results are demonstrated.
- A continuous cycle of improvement is followed.

In order to ensure effective TQM implementation and sustained quality improvement levels, a complete cultural transformation is essential. Following are some of the key factors to be considered:

- Ensure that management is truly committed and demonstrates its commitment across the entire organization.
- Develop open, responsive, group-driven quality leadership.
- Continuously reassert that quality is everyone's responsibility and not just that of a few key people. There is a need to be obsessed with quality and excellence.
- Strike out a balance between long-term goals and successive short-term objectives. Establish a sense of constancy of purpose and a focus on long-term continuous improvement.
- Use a systematic approach and disciplined methodology to clearly understand the external and internal customer requirements. Make the organization customer satisfaction driven.
- Establish a mutually supportive control and improvement partnership with the suppliers.
- Use process improvement teams to involve everyone and seek improvement ideas and opportunities.
- Recognize employee achievement and establish an effective incentive program.
- Institute a continuous process of education, training, learning and self-improvement.
- Ensure that the emphasis on customer focus and continuous improvement permeates the whole organization.

These key considerations can be summarized as the ten commandments of TQM, as given in Table 4.

Table 4. TQM: The Ten Commandments
1. Total Management Commitment
2. Obsession with Excellence
3. Constancy of Purpose
4. Customer-Driven Organization
5. Supplier Partnering
6. Employee Involvement/Empowerment
7. Recognition and Incentive
8. Disciplined Methodology
9. Continuous Learning
10. Continuous Improvement

THREE

TQM MODEL VIA ISO 9004

◆ INTRODUCTION

The International Organization for Standardization (ISO) through one of its technical committees, ISO/TC 176: Quality Management and Quality Assurance, has developed a series (known as the ISO-9000 series) of quality system standards (see Chapter 8). In this series, ISO-9004: Quality Management and Quality System Elements - Guidelines provides guidelines for developing and implementing a TQM System.

Therefore, ISO-9004 provides an alternative approach for an enterprise to establish a TQM System. Companies who intend on seeking quality system certification to the ISO-9000 series may find it beneficial to utilize the ISO-9004 approach in developing a TQM model.

◆ PREMISE OF ISO-9004

The document addresses the aspects of quality management system in relation to a company's needs and interests as well as to a customer's needs and expectations. For the company, there is a business need to achieve quality at optimum cost and to ensure profitability, expanded market share and survivability. The enterprise, however, must understand that there are risks and costs associated with the production of deficient products and services, including loss of reputation/credibility, loss of markets, complaints, liability, waste of resources, and costs associated with repair, rework, replacement, reprocessing and warranties.

The customer, on the other hand, needs confidence in the ability of the enterprise to consistently provide high quality products and services. If the enterprise fails to provide the stipulated quality, the customer also suffers risks and associated costs such as those pertaining to loss of confidence, health and safety, availability, marketing claims, and costs associated with safety, acquisition, downtime, maintenance, repair and disposal.

It is, therefore, fundamentally important for a company to implement an effective quality management system to protect its own interests as well as to satisfy the customer's needs and expectations. The system, however, must be developed and implemented with great tenacity and accommodate at least the following characteristics:

- It must be appropriate for the type of activity and for the product or service being offered.
- It must be commensurate with the company's quality policy and objectives.
- The system should include an effective control mechanism to prevent the recurrence of quality deficiencies.

◆ ISO-9004: TQM MODEL

ISO-9004 describes the quality system principles in the form of a "Quality Loop" which encompasses all the activities and phases, from the initial identification through to the final satisfaction of customer requirements and expectations. These phases and activities may include the following:

- Marketing and market research
- Design/specification engineering and product development
- Procurement
- Process planning and development
- Production
- Inspection, testing and examination
- Packaging and storage
- Sales and distribution
- Installation and operation
- Technical assistance and maintenance
- Disposal after use

A detailed checklist of the ISO-9004 system elements is appended in Table 5. The document compartmentalizes the total set of system elements into the following seventeen areas:

1. Management responsibility
2. Quality system principles
3. Economics - quality related cost considerations
4. Quality in marketing
5. Quality in inspection and design
6. Quality in procurement
7. Quality in production
8. Control of production
9. Product verification
10. Control of measuring and test equipment
11. Nonconformity
12. Corrective action
13. Handling and post-production functions
14. Quality documentation and records
15. Personnel
16. Product safety and liability
17. Use of statistical methods

A TQM model can be conveniently developed by appropriately rearranging these system elements commensurate with the type of activity and the nature of the products and services offered by the company. A detailed TQM document or quality manual must be prepared, addressing these system elements and describing the management responsibilities, systems, procedures, processes and methodologies operating in the company. Following is a suggested TQM framework:

- **Quality Management System:** includes all the quality management aspects such as management responsibility, policy, management systems, control systems, cost systems, evaluation systems, improvement systems, market analysis, resource allocation, etc.

- **Quality Control:** comprises all the critical control points and the operational and technical aspects of controlling quality during production.

- **Procurement Quality Assurance:** includes the quality assurance procedures required to ensure a supply of high quality input.

- **Internal Quality Assurance:** contains the in-house assessment procedures to ensure on-line process control and off-line product quality.

- **External Quality Assurance:** provides a contractual quality assurance protocol to ensure to the regulatory authority, the purchaser, or ultimately the consumer, that the delivered product is of high quality.

Table 5. ISO-9004: TQM System Elements - Master Checklist

- **Management responsibilities:** policy, objectives, planning, management system, organizational structure and responsibilities

- **Structure of the quality system:** quality responsibility and authority, organizational structure, resources and personnel, operational procedures

- **Documentation of the quality system:** quality policies and procedures, quality manual, quality plans, quality records

- **Auditing of the quality system:** audit plan, conducting the audit, reporting of audit findings and follow-up

- **Review and evaluation of the quality management system**

- **Quality-related cost considerations:** selecting appropriate elements; collection and analysis of cost data; cost categories: detection, appraisal, prevention, internal failure, external failure; cost reporting to management

- **Quality in marketing:** market analysis, product brief, customer feedback information

- **Quality in specification and design:** design planning and objectives, product testing and measurement, design qualification and validation, design review, design baseline and production review, market readiness review, design change control, design requalification

- **Quality in production:** planning for controlled production; process capability; supplies, utilities and environments

- **Control of production:** material control and traceability, equipment control and maintenance, special processes, documentation, process change control, control of verification status, control of nonconforming material

- **Product verification:** incoming material and equipment, in-process inspection, completed product verification

Table 5. ISO-9004: TQM System Elements - Master Checklist (continued)

- **Quality in procurement:** requirements for specifications and purchase orders, selection of qualified suppliers, agreement on quality assurance, agreement on verification methods, provision for settlement of quality disputes, receiving inspection planning and control, procurement quality records

- **Control of measuring and test equipment:** measurement, controls, elements of control, supplier measurement controls, corrective action, outside testing

- **Nonconformity:** identification, segregation, review, disposition, documentation, prevention of recurrence

- **Corrective action:** assignment of responsibility, evaluation of importance/priority, investigation of possible problems, analysis of problem preventive measures, process control, disposition of nonconforming items, permanent changes

- **Handling and post-production functions:** handling, storage, identification, packaging and delivery; post-sales service; market reporting and product supervision

- **Quality documentation:** specifications, inspection instructions, test procedures, work instructions, quality manual, operational procedures, quality assurance procedures, etc.

- **Quality records:** inspection records, test data, qualification reports, validation reports, audit reports, material review reports, calibration data, quality cost reports, etc.

- **Personnel:** training, qualifications, appraisal, motivation

- **Product safety and liability:** suitable safety standards; declaration of quality, quantity and content; risk warning to user; product traceability for safety assurance

- **Use of statistical methods:** market analysis, process control, conformance/compliance level, process average, data analysis, safety evaluation and risk analysis, statistical sampling procedures, quality control charts, design methodology, performance appraisal

◆ TQM: THE MANAGEMENT PROFILE

The guidelines presented in ISO-9004 can be utilized in a variety of ways to develop a TQM System. This section provides one example of how a company can structure its TQM plan to describe its operations. For each of the elements itemized below, a clear set of instructions must be outlined in a quality manual so as to facilitate an effective implementation of the quality system.

Management Responsibility

- Quality policy
- Quality objectives
- Organizational responsibilities
- Organizational infrastructure
- Resources and personnel

Management Systems

- Operational framework
- Quality plans
- Quality manual
- Quality procedures
- Quality records
- Reporting system
- Communication system
- Management reviews

Control Systems

- Design/specification control
- Material/equipment control
- Process control
- Change/verification control
- Nonconformance control
- Documentation control
- Post-production/servicing control

Cost System

- Operating quality costs: appraisal, failure, prevention
- External quality costs
- Cost reporting system

Evaluation System

- Incoming inspection
- In-process inspection
- Final inspection
- Measurement system
- Performance evaluation
- Problem analysis
- Corrective/preventive action

Quality Improvement System

- Quality awareness program
- Education/training
- Productivity improvement programs
- Employee motivation
- Merit award system

FOUR

TQM MODEL: ADDITIONAL APPROACHES

◆ INTRODUCTION

In addition to the approaches outlined in the preceding two chapters, a TQM model can also be developed based on the philosophies and methodologies set forth by various quality experts. The following are considered in this chapter as methods for deriving a TQM System:

- The Deming Approach
- The Juran Approach
- The Crosby Approach

It should be noted that only a basic framework of these approaches is described here. For serious application of any approach selected from these, the reader is advised to consult other useful sources and references.

◆ TQM SYSTEM: THE DEMING APPROACH

It was in Japan, in 1950, where Dr. W. Edwards Deming first introduced and emphasized the use of statistical quality control methods to improve quality. Later, he developed his 14-point philosophy (see Table 6) for establishing a total quality system. The 14 points do not offer any exotic theory of behaviour, nor any structured set of system elements for establishing a TQM system. They are derived from first-hand observations and, therefore, reflect Deming's insight and experience for improving quality.

Table 6. Dr. Deming's 14 Points

1. Create constancy of purpose for improvement of product and service.

2. Adopt the new philosophy.

3. Cease dependence on inspection to achieve quality.

4. End the practice of awarding business on the basis of price tag alone. Instead, minimize total cost by working with a single supplier.

5. Improve constantly and forever every process for planning, production, and service.

6. Institute training on the job.

7. Adopt and institute leadership.

8. Drive out fear.

9. Break down barriers between staff areas.

10. Eliminate slogans, exhortations, and targets for the work force.

11. Eliminate numerical quotas for the work force and numerical goals for management.

12. Remove barriers that rob people of pride of workmanship. Eliminate the annual rating or merit system.

13. Institute a vigorous program of education and self-improvement for everyone.

14. Put everybody in the company to work to accomplish the transformation.

Deming's 14 points provide a thought-provoking framework for management to come to grips with the realities of the competitive quality revolution and to institute changes and transformations to improve and maintain quality. The most befitting analogy to Deming's concept is the statement made by the late Kaora Ishikawa of Japan, "Quality control is a thought revolution in management". Good quality, according to Deming, means a predictable degree of uniformity and dependability at low cost, with the quality suited to the market. This emphasis is portrayed in Deming's famous chain reaction, given as follows:

Improve Quality → Improve Productivity →
Decrease Costs → Lower Prices → Capture Markets →
Stay in Business → Provide Jobs → Return on Investment

The gist of Deming's 14-point philosophy can be stated as follows:

- Commitment to quality, constancy of purpose
- Effective leadership
- Continuous improvement of products/services
- Reduction/elimination of variability
- Process improvement with statistical methods
- Continuous training/retraining
- Teamwork, effective communication
- Pride in workmanship
- Quality - everyone's business

Although it is not easy to develop a structured TQM System using Deming's philosophy, the following provides a list of essential activities and actions that the management must undertake to develop and implement an effective quality improvement system.

Deming Point #1

- Define the quality mission and vision.
- Define the quality policy, objectives and standards.
- Develop long-range plans.
- Identify management commitment and continued responsibility to quality.
- Develop quality leadership.
- Institute continuous training.
- Put resources into research, education and the maintenance of equipment.
- Innovate and constantly improve the design of the product.
- Command constancy of purpose and dedication.

Deming Point #2

- Bring about management transformation and accept the challenge of doing things right the first time.
- Constantly review and analyze the systems and related quality procedures.
- Replace inadequate supervision with leadership.
- Teach, develop skills and abandon the mentality that permits an acceptable level of deficiency.

Deming Point #3

- Quality cannot be inspected in; it has to be manufactured in.
- Reduce dependence on mass inspection to achieve quality.
- Achieve quality through process control.
- Produce right in the first place.

Deming Point #4

- Select suppliers based on their ability to provide quality material and services rather than on the price tag.
- Establish a long-term partnership with the suppliers.
- Establish a process control and improvement system with the suppliers.

Deming Point #5

- Continuously hunt for areas to be improved: procurement, design, production, data collection, measurement system, customer satisfaction, employee involvement, etc.
- Constantly improve the system of production and services. Use Deming's continuous quality improvement cycle, PDSA - Plan, Do, Study, Act.
- Understand variation and its causes. Use statistical process control methods to eliminate deficiencies and improve processes.

Deming Point #6

- Institute modern methods of training on the job.
- Train workers in the concepts of Statistical Process Control (SPC) to improve processes.
- Provide employee training opportunities in new and effective techniques.
- Set standards for new recruits.
- Establish a schedule for continuous training.

Deming Point #7

- The traditional dictatorial supervisory role must change to a proactive leadership role.

- Make the organization flexible so that supervisors may become part of the quality team.
- The new supervisor is responsible for ensuring that quality action is taken in all areas impacting quality.

Deming Point #8

- Create a management environment where people feel secure, confident, responsible and fulfilled.
- Everyone in the organization should be able to express ideas/opinions, ask questions, suggest system deficiencies and improvements, and have pride in their workmanship.
- Create a climate of trust and openness.
- The management must be open-minded and responsive to suggestions.

Deming Point #9

- Break down inter and intra-departmental barriers.
- Establish a cross-functional interface to encourage communication.
- Establish a well-coordinated and integrated system.
- Institute a participative team approach.
- Try to eliminate or minimize psychological and emotional barriers to job performance such as: jealousy, ambition, fear, personality conflicts, fear of change, etc.

Deming Point #10

- Eliminate arbitrary goals and slogans.
- Do not judge performance by numbers. Instead, encourage people to be productive and innovative.
- Do not set targets that may cause workers to compromise and make sacrifices at the altar of quality.

Deming Point #11

- Eliminate work standards that prescribe numerical quotas.
- Eliminate those goals and objectives that hinder performance.
- Learn, teach and institute methods of process improvement.

Deming Point #12

- Eliminate inhibitors (physical, environmental, psychological, emotional) to the improvement of quality and productivity.
- Involve and empower people to do the job well.
- Remove barriers that stand between workers and their pride of workmanship.

Deming Point #13

- Identify training needs and institute a vigorous program of education and self-improvement.
- Emphasize and encourage educational opportunities.
- Create a climate of personal growth and achievement.
- Train employees in statistical methods used for process improvement.

Deming Point #14

- Create a dedicated and committed management structure that will make the transformation succeed.
- Create a quality culture.
- Make people responsible for and proud of their work.
- Recognize achievement.
- Make quality everyone's business.

Deming: Theory of Profound Knowledge

To further elucidate his 14-point theory, Deming has identified what he calls "a system of profound knowledge", the understanding of which he considers imperative for the effective implementation of a TQM System. The essential elements of this system include:

- **Knowledge of Variation**

  - Understand the role of variation.
  - Improve processes by reducing/eliminating variability.
  - Use statistical process control methods to control, monitor and improve processes.

- **Knowledge of Loss Function**

  - Identify critical quality characteristics and their associated costs.
  - Identify costs/losses incurred due to poor quality by the organization, by the customer or through sub-optimization.
  - Improve quality by minimizing/optimizing costs.

- **Knowledge of Win-Win Philosophy**

  - Success comes through cooperation rather than competition.
  - Establish a partnership with the suppliers and customers.

- **Knowledge of Psychology**

  - Understand the role of intrinsic and extrinsic motivation.
  - Understand the psychology of change.
  - Involve and empower the workforce.
  - Create a joy of work.
  - Improve inter/intra-communication.

- **Knowledge of Reliability**

  - Understand the operational functionality of the system.
  - Improve the dependability of the system.
  - Emphasize product performance rather than just the intended design or usage.

- **Theory of Knowledge**

  - Understand the organizational operational and communication systems.
  - Understand the theory of prediction.
  - Use theory and experience together.
  - Obtain data.
  - Use statistical methods for analyzing information for effective decision-making.

◆ TQM SYSTEM: THE JURAN APPROACH

Dr. Joseph M. Juran is another famous quality expert with a powerful message. The basic premise of Juran's philosophy can be summarized as follows:

- Quality means fitness for use.
- Quality holds the key to competitive survivability.
- There is a new world order for quality. To do business in this new Quality-Productivity Era would require excellence in the quality of products and services.
- Quality improvement requires relinquishing the traditional approaches and charting a new course with the following attributes:
  - Constancy in improvement, ie., an ongoing annual improvement in quality, year after year
  - Hands-on leadership by upper management
  - A universal way of thinking about quality, ie., a quality culture that permeates and applies to all levels of the organization.

- Establishment of new policies, goals, plans, organizational measures and controls throughout the organization. These quality management measures and activities must be designed with great care so as to allow a smooth transition and acceptance within the company.
- Creation of cross-functional unity in the organization so that everyone will be aware of the new directions
- Massive training in quality at all levels of the organization

The basic components of the TQM System, according to Juran, involve quality planning, quality control and quality improvement. The elements of this trilogy as outlined by Dr. Juran are appended in Table 7.

The planning process is essential for delineating a quality road map. It prepares the company to meet and achieve quality goals. A well-planned process is always capable of meeting quality goals under operating conditions. Some of the basic elements of quality planning involve the following:

- Identifying the customer requirements
- Developing the product vis-à-vis these requirements
- Identifying the processes that impact quality
- Establishing quality goals
- Ensuring process capability to meet these quality goals

Quality control activities ensure that the conduct of operations is in accordance with the stipulated quality plans and procedures. A well-controlled production process is guaranteed to yield a consistently high quality product that is predictable, reliable, fit for use, and meeting the customer's needs and requirements. Quality control activities involve the following elements:

- Identifying the areas requiring controls
- Implementing control procedures
- Establishing a measurement system
- Setting performance standards
- Measuring actual against expected performance
- Taking action on the deviations

Quality improvement activities lead a company towards excellence and provide a competitive edge. They realize unprecedented levels of performance that achieve customer delight. Continuous quality improvement is the key to expan-

Table 7. Basic Quality Process: Juran

Quality Planning

Identify the customers, both external and internal.
Determine customer needs.
Develop product features that respond to customer needs. (Products include both goods and services.)
Establish quality goals that meet the needs of customers and suppliers alike, and do so at a minimum combined cost.
Develop a process that can produce the needed product features.
Prove process capability - prove that the process can meet the quality goals under operating conditions.

Quality Control

Choose control subjects - what to control.
Choose units of measurement.
Establish measurement.
Establish standards of performance.
Measure actual performance.
Interpret the difference (actual versus standard).
Take action on the difference.

Quality Improvement

Prove the need for improvement.
Identify specific projects for improvement.
Organize to guide the projects.
Organize for diagnosis - for discovery of causes.
Diagnose to find the causes.
Provide remedies.
Prove that the remedies are effective under operating conditions.
Provide for control to hold the gains.

ded markets, higher profits and long-term survival. Quality improvement activities include the following:

- Determining improvement needs, opportunities and initiatives
- Identifying specific projects for improvement
- Establishing improvement teams
- Implementing improvement strategies
- Identifying deficiencies
- Instituting remedial measures
- Assessing improvement
- Controlling the processes to maintain gains.

A careful and systematic implementation of the elements identified above would result in an effective TQM System. For a more serious application and use of Juran's methods, the reader is advised to consult other appropriate sources and references.

◆ TQM SYSTEM: THE CROSBY APPROACH

Philip B. Crosby, another well-known quality management expert, bases his approach to implementing a TQM System on his "Four Absolutes of Quality" and his 14-step implementation plan. The four absolutes are:

- The definition of quality is conformance to requirements.
- The system of quality is prevention.
- The performance standard is zero defects.
- The measurement of quality is the price of nonconformance.

Crosby's 14-step plan, appended in Table 8, needs careful understanding and interpretation for an effective TQM System implementation. The basic premise of Crosby's approach is as follows:

Step 1: Management Commitment

- Management must display personal commitment and participation in the quality program.
- Define and establish the quality policy and objectives.
- Make sure that the policy and commitment is understood, implemented and maintained at all levels of the organization.

Table 8. The Fourteen Steps: Crosby

1. Management Commitment

2. Quality Improvement Team

3. Measurement

4. Cost of Quality

5. Quality Awareness

6. Corrective Action

7. Zero Defects Planning

8. Education

9. Zero Defects Day

10. Goal Setting

11. Error Cause Removal

12. Recognition

13. Quality Councils

14. Do It Over Again

Reproduced with permission of Philip Crosby Associates, Inc. © 1991
"The Creative Factory, Inc."

Step 2: Quality Improvement Team

- Establish an inter/intra-departmental and cross-functional quality improvement team.
- The team must clearly understand the task at hand and should have all the necessary tools to do the job.

Step 3: Measurement

- Establish a formal and well-structured quality measurement system/procedures for all areas of activity. Revise/review these procedures as appropriate.
- Measurement data should be properly recorded.
- The quality improvement status should be identified.
- Corrective action should be taken where required.
- Make use of charts to identify and display the quality improvement results.

Step 4: Cost of Quality

- Establish a quality cost system. Evaluate the total costs necessary to achieve the desired quality.
- Use the cost data to optimize the corrective action strategy.

Step 5: Quality Awareness

- Foster quality awareness programs.
- Educate the employees on the:
  - Costs of poor quality
  - Concern for quality improvement
  - Positive attitude towards quality
  - Importance of quality related discussions, interface and cross-functional dialogue

Step 6: Corrective Action

- Quality awareness, attitude and discussions lead to the identification of quality problems and opportunities for corrective action.
- Quality problems should be identified at the team meetings and appropriate corrective action should be initiated.

Step 7: Zero Defects Planning

- The emphasis should be on doing things right the first time.
- Establish a Zero Defects program and make sure that everyone clearly understands its purpose, scope and importance. Ensure the complete participation of everyone.
- Identify improvements made through the program and repeat the continuous cycle.

Step 8: Education

- Identify the total training needs at all levels of the organization.
- Provide appropriate education and training in each area of activity.

Step 9: Zero Defects Day

- Establish a formal Zero Defects Day.
- Emphasize the company's commitment to the Zero Defects program.
- Explain the Zero Defects program to everyone and expound it as the company's performance standard.

Step 10: Goal Setting

- Encourage employees to set up short-term and long-term goals for themselves.
- The goals should be specific and measurable.
- Employees should be encouraged to monitor their performance and progress in realizing their goals.

Step 11: Error Cause Removal

- Establish a system whereby employees can identify problems that hinder performing their work without deficiencies.
- Ensure that appropriate functional groups continuously provide prompt solutions and remedies to these designated problems.

Step 12: Recognition

- Establish a viable system to recognize the outstanding achievements of employees.
- The prizes and awards should not be financial in nature but rather serve as expressions of praise and appreciation.

Step 13: Quality Councils

- Establish councils comprised of quality professionals and team chairpersons.
- Schedule regular council meetings to study the efficacy of the quality program, to identify the system's strengths and weaknesses and to generate continuous improvement strategies.

Step 14: Do It Over Again

- Most programs tend to loose their drive, prowess and impact over extended periods of time. Every so often, at appropriate intervals, re-energize the quality program by doing it all over again.
- Maintain a continuous cycle of improvement.

◆ TQM: THE JAPANESE PERSPECTIVE

For the sake of comparison, let us briefly outline the Japanese approach to quality. Japanese-style total quality control is referenced by the phrase "Company-Wide Quality Control" (CWQC) and is a bit broader in scope than its U.S. counterpart. The late Karoa Ishikawa, one of the leading pioneers of quality control in Japan, has defined and differentiated the U.S. and Japanese styles of total quality control as follows:

> **"Total Quality Control (TQC):** A system for integrating quality technologies into various functional departments (ie., engineering, production, sales and service) to achieve customer satisfaction."

> **"Company-Wide Quality Control (CWQC):** A means to provide good and low cost products, dividing the benefits among consumers, employees, and stockholders while improving the quality of people's lives."

The Japanese emphasis of quality is on customer satisfaction and value for money. This is evidenced by the definition of quality control given in the Japanese Industrial Standard Z8101-1981:

> **"Quality Control:** A system of means to economically produce goods or services which satisfy the customer's requirements."

Some of the key characteristics of the Japanese approach to quality can be summarized as follows:

- "Quality control is a thought revolution in management" - Ishikawa
- While the North American emphasis is limited to the product, process and system, the Japanese approach goes further to also include a focus on cost, employee involvement, customer satisfaction and welfare of society at large.
- Specifically, the Japanese approach puts greater onus on:
  - Design improvement
  - Extensive testing
  - Higher production levels
  - No compromise on quality
  - Extensive internal auditing
  - Total employee involvement
  - Problem-solving

- Use of statistical methods
- Partnering with suppliers and customers

◆ THE TQM EPILOGUE

Whatever method, approach or philosophy may be used to achieve quality, it would be unrealistic to expect quality to spring up overnight with a big bang. Quality comes through small increments, step by step, piece by piece. Since quality is fundamental to improved profitability, credibility, marketability, growth and survival, the two quality imperatives are then:

- **Customer Focus:** total customer satisfaction/delight by meeting/exceeding their requirements/expectations.
- **Long-Term Total Quality Focus:** concern for the quality of all aspects of the organization with constancy of purpose. This involves supplier-customer partnering; employee involvement, empowerment, and recognition; quality of processes, procedures, products and services; etc.

Briefly summarizing our discussion on quality, the following axiomatic commonalities may be worthy of recapitulation:

- **Management Responsibilities/Action**

  - Management to display active commitment and leadership.
  - Management to identify a committed mission, vision, quality policy/objectives.
  - Management to inspire a shared vision, model the way, be approachable, enable and encourage everyone to contribute, act and achieve.
  - The quality policy and strategy to be clear, simple, direct and applicable to all.
  - The quality organization to be supportive of quality activities and inter/intra-communication and interfacing.
  - Total cross-functional coordination is required between sales, marketing, design, procurement, production, and other administrative/organizational elements.

- **Supplier-Customer Partnering**

  - Creating trust and a lasting relationship with suppliers
  - Effectively communicating requirements to suppliers with continued mutual input into each other's process control activities

- Clearly understanding customer's requirements, expectations, and service standards
- Seeking total customer commitment, satisfaction and partnering

- **Employee Involvement**

  - Totally integrated work environment
  - Participative management: Steering Committee, Process Improvement Teams, etc.
  - Employee empowerment, recognition and rewards
  - Free and open inter/intra-functional communication and coordination.
  - Management concern for employee welfare, pride of workmanship and quality of work-life

- **Disciplined and Structured Systems**

  - Process control and management
  - Improvement projects
  - Effective measurement, evaluation and verification systems
  - Education and training

Total quality improvement is a game collectively played by four teams of players: the suppliers, customers, management and employees. The game may be played in any number of ways but the result must be the same: all four teams as winners; there must not be any losers. Quality is a win-win game.

FIVE

SERVICE QUALITY MODEL

◆ SERVICE QUALITY

A large proportion of our industrial infrastructure comprises service organizations yet very little is discussed about managing the quality of services. This incongruity may perhaps be due to our:

- Excessive preoccupation with quality of manufactured products.
- Difficulty in defining roles and functions of a service.
- Inability to define service quality characteristics.
- Lack of knowledge and expertise for developing a service TQM model.
- Assumptions that service quality is of secondary importance.

The trends and activities in the domain of quality have undergone tremendous changes during the past two decades. There is a market-driven quality revolution and its impact is now being felt equally in the manufacturing and the service sectors. While demanding high quality products at competitive prices, the customers are also expecting excellence in services. Service quality management has taken on a new perspective and there is an ever increasing interest in service quality improvement.

What is a service? Basically, a service can be defined as an activity that does not produce a product. The international standard ISO/CD 8402-1 defines a service as:

> "**Service:** The results generated by activities at the interface between the supplier and the customer and by the supplier's internal activities, to meet the customer needs."

The following "notes" also accompany this definition in the standard:

- The supplier or the customer may be represented at the interface by personnel or equipment.
- Customer activities at the interface with the supplier may be essential to the service delivery.
- Delivery or use of tangible products may form part of the service delivery.
- A service may be linked with the manufacture and supply of tangible product.

Service quality implies the quality of the internal as well as external processes that lead to providing services that meet the customer's needs and requirements. Generally, service quality is referenced with respect to the following two situations:

- Service that is directly related to a tangible entity or product, ie., the after-sales servicing function associated with the sale of a manufactured product
- Service that is solely an intangible service entity with little or no product involved

The quality aspects of product-related servicing function, being an integral part of any product-oriented TQM System, has been adequately covered in the preceding chapters. In this chapter, we shall outline the development and implementation of a TQM System as applicable to organizations that are involved solely in the provision of intangible services. Some examples of such services are: banks, department stores, large scale retailers, hotels, restaurants, taxis, airlines, amusement clubs, communications, health, education, financial, legal and consulting services, etc.

♦ SERVICE QUALITY CHARACTERISTICS

Although the basic principles of quality management are universally applicable to manufacturing as well as service operations, services have some unique and special characteristics that must be carefully taken into consideration when developing a service TQM model. Some of these special features may include the following:

- Services are intangible even when they may involve tangible products.
- Services are personalized.
- Services also involve the customer to whom service is being delivered.
- Services are produced on demand.
- Services cannot be manufactured prior to delivery.
- Services are produced and consumed at the same time.
- Services cannot be shown or exhibited prior to delivery.
- Services are perishable; they cannot be stored or stocked.
- Services cannot be inspected or tested.
- Services do not produce defects, scrap or rejects.
- Service quality deficiencies cannot be eliminated before delivery.
- Services cannot be substituted or sold as second choice.
- Services are labour-intensive; they may involve complex cross-functional integration of several support systems.

◆ SERVICE QUALITY DIMENSIONS

Measuring and evaluating the quality of manufactured products is not so difficult. Standards of conformance can be set, products can be inspected and tested, defective rates can be identified, deficiencies can be corrected, and performance levels can be established.

In comparison, service quality performance is hard to measure because services are intangible, perishable and subjective in nature. It is the customer who decides what constitutes a quality service. The customer generally bases his evaluation process on such characteristics as: his image, expectations, and perceptions about quality; the way the service is delivered; the end result of the service; and the extent of his satisfaction. Most of these characteristics are hard to quantify. Measuring service quality, therefore, poses a phenomenal challenge - anticipating customer's wants, needs and expectations for something that is intangible, involves the customer himself, cannot be seen or tested, and may be judged on purely subjective idiosyncratic basis.

Another difficulty with evaluating service quality is that there are no standards against which to measure performance. Service quality standards are difficult to establish because service is subjectively measurable and every customer has his or her own set of expectations and perspectives about what constitutes a quality service.

Despite the obvious difficulties in measuring, evaluating or standardizing quality service performance, however, the following attributes are considered essential
to service operations:

- Efficiency, accuracy
- Consistency, constancy
- Responsiveness, approachability
- Dependability, reliability
- Competence, capability
- Safety, security
- Courtesy, care, understanding
- Price, affordability
- Satisfaction, delight

Commensurate with these quality dimensions, we can outline some of the key
factors in a customer's expectations of a quality treatment:

- Prompt attention
- Understanding of what the customer wants
- Complete and undivided attention
- Courteous and polite treatment
- Expression of interest in the customer
- Responsiveness to a query
- Expression of proactive helpfulness
- Efficiency in the delivery of service
- Accuracy in the end result of service
- Explanation of procedures
- Expression of pleasure in serving the customer
- Expression of thanks
- Attention to complaints
- Resolution of complaints to the customer's satisfaction
- Acceptance of responsibility for personal or company errors

◆ DEVELOPING A SERVICE TQM MODEL

Quality system implementation is relatively easier in the manufacturing situations because all the processes involved in the production of the product are
clearly identifiable. All that remains to be done is to delineate responsibilities,
allocate resources and establish appropriate systems, procedures and processes.

The sequence of steps in the production cycle are systematic and everyone has a clearly well-defined and distinct role to play.

The situation with service industries is, however, not as simple. The process steps may be identifiable, but the collective cross-functional integration and understanding of each other's roles and functions may not be evident. The customer, for example, does not buy from the CEO, the manager or the owner. The customer's contact is limited to the front desk, the salesperson who is actually delivering the service. These and only these persons typically determine the quality of the service rendered. The management may not even be aware of the actual service quality level. Thus, in the case of service operations, a well coordinated process improvement system has to be established and the entire infrastructure of the organization has to be involved.

Like any manufacturing situation, continuous service quality improvement also requires the implementation of an integrated total quality system. The basic framework of a service TQM model is no different from that for the manufactured products. Therefore, any of the methods and approaches outlined in earlier chapters can be applied, with appropriate modifications, to develop the system. A typical service TQM model is suggested here in Table 9. The main elements of the model almost follow the same sequence as the generic TQM model described earlier in Chapter 2.

Table 9. Service TQM Model
Step 1: Customer Needs Step 2: Management Responsibility Step 3: Service Processes Step 4: Improvement Projects Step 5: Continuous Improvement Step 6: Evaluation Step 7: Review/Revision

Step 1: Customer Needs

- Define and identify customer needs and requirements.
- Develop a system to identify customer's expectations.
- Identify customer's perspective relating to:
  - Service quality characteristics/attributes
  - Service delivery attributes
  - Service end result expectations
  - Satisfaction criteria
- Use all possible means to obtain customer's input: surveys, questionnaires, observations, mail/personal/telephone interviews, complaints, etc.

Step 2: Management Responsibility

- Identify the nature of your service.
- Identify all the processes that collectively make up the service.
- Identify the service competency vis-à-vis customer's needs.
- Identify service deficiencies.
- Identify the activities and actions needed to eliminate deficiencies to satisfy customer requirements.
- Define your mission.
- Establish policies, objectives, goals.
- Develop a quality improvement plan.
- Establish improvement infrastructure: process improvement teams, steering committee.
- Identify your suppliers and subcontractors.
- Identify the supplier's strengths and weaknesses.
- Establish a partnership with the suppliers.

Step 3: Service Processes

- Identify all the processes involved in the service.
- Define process goals and priorities.
- Define process requirements and boundaries.
- Flow chart the processes.
- Evaluate process capability.
- Identify improvement opportunities.

Step 4: Improvement Projects

- Establish and implement improvement projects.
- Establish a measurement system to assess performance.
- Report the quality and service information data.

Step 5: Continuous Improvement

- Collect data to analyze the processes and projects.
- Review reports and performance levels.
- Analyze the nature and extent of errors, trends and quality costs.
- Institute appropriate corrective/preventive measures.
- Monitor implementation.
- Assess improvements made.
- Identify further improvement opportunities.
- Develop strategic initiatives.
- Implement additional improvement projects.

Step 6: Evaluation

- Establish audit/evaluation procedures.
- Identify the system's strengths and weaknesses.
- Audit the procedural compliance.
- Monitor the data integrity.
- Take appropriate management decisions.

Step 7: Review/Revision

- Repeat the continuous improvement cycle.

As indicated above, there are two elements that require special attention in a service quality operation:

- Obtaining customer input
- Improving performance of the persons directly in contact with and responsible for delivering the service to the customer

A continuous evaluation of the customer's needs, requirements and perception about service quality is fundamentally important for profitability and competitive survival. All possible means should be utilized to obtain customer's input. It is essential to know what characteristics of the service pleases or displeases a customer. This information is vitally important to institute any measure of process improvement.

Secondly, as indicated above, customers do not buy from the CEOs. They buy or are serviced by individuals who do the work: salespersons, repair persons, telephone clerks, bank tellers, waiters, etc. These are the people who determine the quality of the service rendered. For quality performance, these persons must possess as a minimum the following traits:

- Courtesy
- Competency
- Accuracy
- Reliability
- Responsiveness
- Patience
- Maturity
- Ability to listen to a customer

To improve quality at this level, effective management-directed motivational programs must be established, such as:

- Manpower planning and career development
- Continuous training and development
- Motivation program
- Employee involvement, empowerment and suggestion system
- Defect prevention program
- Incentive program

◆ SERVICE TQM MODEL VIA ISO 9004-2

Another excellent source of information for developing a service TQM model is the International Standard: "ISO 9004-2 (1991): Quality Management and Quality System Elements - Part 2: Guidelines for Services." This standard is a useful addition to the ISO-9000 series and has been prepared on the same basic quality management principles as given in the ISO-9000 to ISO-9004 series of international standards. In this section, we shall only present a basic framework of the systems elements as outlined in ISO-9004-2. For more extensive applications, the reader is advised to consult the document.

The basic steps for developing a total quality system for services involve the following:

- Defining and identifying service quality characteristics and a service delivery mechanism.
- Establishing management responsibilities and infrastructure.

- Establishing a quality system structure.
- Planning and developing operational procedures.
- Establishing service performance evaluation procedures.
- Developing improvement strategies.

Service Quality Characteristics

- Identify service requirements in terms of the customer's perspectives, expectations or characteristics by which the customer evaluates the service quality.
- Identify the service delivery characteristics.
- Establish an effective service delivery system.
- Monitor, control and evaluate the delivery process.

Management Responsibilities

- Identify and document quality policies, goals and objectives.
- Define the company's mission.
- Develop appropriate service quality infrastructure.
- Assign quality responsibilities and authority.
- Establish quality steering committee and process improvement teams.
- Allocate appropriate personnel, material and financial resources.
- Establish training and development programs.
- Establish a management review process for the quality system.

Quality System Structure

- Establish appropriate procedures, processes and projects.
- Develop a documentation system including a:
  - Quality manual
  - Quality plan
  - Quality procedures
  - Quality records
- Establish a documentation review/change control process.
- Establish internal quality audit procedures.
- Interface with customers by:
  - Ensuring continuous communication with customers.
  - Obtaining customer input.
  - Monitoring/controlling service quality vis-à-vis the customer's perspectives.
  - Establishing a partnership with customers.

Operational Procedures/Processes

(This step applies to the Marketing Process, Design Process and Delivery Process.)

- Identify the customer's needs and expectations.
- Identify the company's capabilities.
- Develop a road map for implementing the service.
- Prepare a service brief.
- Prepare a marketing/advertising strategy.
- Design the service.
- Establish a service delivery process.
- Flow chart the process.
- Assess the delivery process.
- Obtain the customer's assessment on services rendered.
- Update the service status.
- Identify deficiencies and take corrective action.
- Establish a measurement system.
- Establish a monitoring and control system.

Evaluation Procedures

- Collect data and information.
- Analyze data, using statistical methods.
- Identify errors, omissions, deficiencies.
- Take corrective/preventive action.

Continuous Improvement

- Continuously review/revise processes.
- Develop improvement strategies and initiatives.
- Implement improvement projects.
- Commit to continuous improvement.

SIX

SOFTWARE QUALITY MODEL

◆ INTRODUCTION

If there is any field that has witnessed the most rapid growth in the least amount of time, it is that of "information technology". As a result, the amount of software products have also been increasing at a considerable rate. To ensure software quality, there is a need to establish guidelines for developing and implementing a quality management system. The technical committee, ISO/TC 176, has developed the following document in the ISO-9000 series which can be gainfully used to develop a software TQM model:

> "**ISO-9000-3 (1991)**: Quality Management and Quality Assurance Standards - Part 3: Guidelines for the Application of ISO-9001 to the Development, Supply and Maintenance of Software."

In this chapter we shall briefly outline the basic framework for developing a software TQM model on the basis of the guidelines appended in ISO-9000-3. For a more extensive coverage of the subject, the reader is advised to consult the document. The document has been based on the underlying quality system requirement of ISO-9001. However, since the process of development and maintenance of software is different from that of most other types of industrial products, appropriate modifications have been incorporated to accommodate the quality aspects related to software technology.

◆ ISO 9000-3: TQM SYSTEM ELEMENTS

The basic definition of "software" as given in "ISO 9000-3" and "ISO-2382/1: Data Processing - Vocabulary, Part 1: Fundamental Terms" is as follows:

> **"Software:** Intellectual creation comprising the programs, procedures, rules and any associated documentation pertaining to the operation of a *data processing system."*

NOTE: Software is independent of the carrier used for transport.

The overall systems elements for developing a software quality assurance model as outlined in ISO-9000-3 are as follows:

Quality System - Framework

- Management responsibility
- Quality system
- Internal quality system audits
- Corrective action

Quality System - Life Cycle Activities

- Contract reviews
- Purchaser's requirements specification
- Development planning
- Quality planning
- Design and implementation
- Testing and validation
- Acceptance
- Replication, delivery and installation
- Maintenance

Quality System - Supporting Activities

- Configuration management
- Document control
- Quality records
- Measurements
- Rules, practices and conventions
- Tools and techniques
- Purchasing
- Included software product
- Training

◆ DEVELOPING A SOFTWARE TQM MODEL

As indicated in the preceding chapters, the initial steps in the development of a TQM System involves strategic planning, preparation and quality orientation. The process should start as follows:

- Develop a mission statement.
- Establish a TQM Steering Committee.
- Identify the quality objectives.
- Identify the processes involved in the software production life cycle.
- Establish Process Improvement Teams.
- Delineate appropriate responsibilities and authority.
- Identify customer requirements.
- Translate customer requirements into specific tasks and projects.
- Develop a quality manual.
- Develop procedures manuals.

The next step involves the identification and implementation of all the requisite quality systems elements. Following is a brief description of the systems elements as outlined in ISO-9000-3.

Quality System - Framework

Management Responsibility

- Establish a quality policy, goals and objectives.
- Establish a quality infrastructure with appropriate responsibilities and authority.
- Identify the requisite verification resources and personnel.
- Appoint a management representative to oversee the effective implementation of the quality system.
- Establish a management review process to ensure the continuing suitability and effectiveness of the quality system.
- Establish a partnership with the customer to:
  - Achieve continuous feedback - feedforward.
  - Ensure conformance of the software to the customer's agreed requirements specification.
  - Verify/accept test results.

Quality System

- Establish, maintain and document an effective and integrated quality system that spans over the entire life cycle of the software production and ensures total quality.
- Document the quality system via a quality manual, procedural manuals, work instructions, etc.
- Establish a quality plan.

Internal Quality System Audits

- Establish an effective internal quality audit system to verify the quality system's effectiveness and the product conformance status.
- Take appropriate corrective action on the deficiencies identified by the audit.

Corrective Action

- Establish procedures to investigate causes of nonconforming product.
- Analyze quality records and information to detect and eliminate deficiencies.
- Apply controls to ensure that appropriate and timely corrective/preventive actions are taken and that they are effective.

Quality System - Life Cycle Activities

Contract Reviews

- Establish effective contract review procedures. The supplier should review each contract to ensure that:
  - Requirements are properly defined and documented.
  - Possible risks are identified.
  - Any discrepancies are resolved.
  - The supplier has the capability to meet the requirements.
  - The purchaser has the capability to meet contractual obligations.
- Review the contract to ensure that it adequately addresses all the requisite criteria for the acceptance and handling of changes and problems, standards/procedures to be used, and the purchaser's responsibilities with regard to the requirements specification, installation, facilities, tools and software to be provided.

Purchaser's Requirements Specification

- The company (supplier) should ensure that all functional requirements for software development have been obtained from the customer. Some of

these relate to performance, safety, reliability, security and privacy.
- The purchaser's requirements specification must be properly documented. The document must clearly establish and identify the appropriate responsibilities of both the supplier and the purchaser, the methods of approval for the requirements and any ensuing changes, the review procedures, the interfaces between the software product and other software or hardware products, etc.

Development Planning

- Establish a software development plan to include:
  - Project definition, objectives
  - Project organization details: resources, teams, responsibilities, subcontractors to be used, human resources, etc.
  - Project phases: development phases, required input and output for each phase, verification procedures, potential problem analysis strategy and procedures, etc.
  - Project schedule
  - Identification of requisite plans: quality plan, configuration management plan, integration plan, test plan
  - Identification of how the project will be managed
  - Development methods and tools
  - Progress control procedures
  - Documentation of inputs and outputs from each development phase
  - Verification procedures for each phase.

Quality Planning

- Establish and document a quality plan to describe the road map for the development and progress of each phase of the software development process.
- The quality plan should identify the:
  - Quality objective
  - Defined input and output criteria for each phase of the development process.
  - Details of the test verification and validation activities.
  - Specific quality responsibilities, ie., reviews and tests, configuration management and change control, defect control and corrective action, etc.

Design and Implementation

- Establish a well-structured and disciplined procedure for the software design and implementation.
- The design activities should include:
  - Proper design rules and internal interface

- Systematic design methodology appropriate to the type of software product being developed
- Use of past design experiences
- Design implementation activities should be in accordance with the established rules, such as the programming rules, programming languages, consistent naming and coding conventions, etc.
- Appropriate implementation methods should be used to satisfy the customer requirements.
- Establish appropriate design review procedures.

Testing and Validation

- Establish effective procedures for testing, validation, and field testing of the software products at each stage of their development.

Acceptance

- A well-defined procedure for acceptance of the final product must be established between the supplier and the purchaser.
- The acceptance procedure should take into consideration the time schedule, the procedures for evaluation, the software/hardware environments and resources, and the acceptance criteria.

Replication, Delivery and Installation

- The supplier must establish criteria for replication prior to delivery. This includes the:
  - Number of copies of each software item to be delivered
  - Copyright and licensing concerns
  - Custody of the master and backup copies
  - Period of obligation for the supplier to supply copies
- Establish appropriate procedures for verifying the correctness and completeness of all copies of the delivered software product.
- The procedures for installation must be clearly established between the supplier and the purchaser.

Maintenance

- The supplier should establish procedures for maintenance of the software if required by the contract.
- Maintenance activities involve problem resolution, interface modification, and the functional expansion of performance improvement.
- Items to be maintained may include programs, data and their structures, specifications, documents for purchase and/or use, and documents for the supplier's use.

- To effectively carry out maintenance activities, the supplier should establish an appropriate maintenance plan that would encompass such activities and factors as the scope of maintenance, the identification of the initial status of the product, the support organizations, the maintenance activities and the maintenance records and reports.
- Maintenance records and reports must be kept.
- The supplier and the purchaser must establish and document procedures for incorporating changes in the software product resulting from the need to maintain performance.

Quality System - Supporting Activities

Configuration Management

- The supplier should develop a configuration management plan and establish an appropriate system for identifying, controlling and tracking the previous versions of each software item.
- Configuration management activities may include configuration identification and traceability, the change control procedures, and the procedures for recording the status report of the software items.

Document Control

- The supplier should establish a document control system.
- Document control applies to such items as procedural documents, planning documents and product documents.
- Procedures should be established for document approval and issue and for changes to documents.

Quality Records

- The supplier should establish and maintain procedures for the identification, collection, indexing, filing, storage, maintenance and disposition of quality records.

Measurements

- As far as possible, the supplier should endeavour to develop quantitative means for measuring the quality of software products and the quality of the development and delivery processes.

Rules, Practices and Conventions

- The supplier should clearly identify the rules, practices and conventions employed in the established quality system.

Tools and Techniques

* The supplier should identify and use appropriate tools and techniques for the effective management of the quality system.

Purchasing

* The supplier should ensure that the purchased products or services conform to the specified requirements. To do so, the subcontractors must be effectively assessed and the purchased products verified and validated.

Included Software Product

* Where a supplier is required to include or use software products supplied by the purchaser or by a third party, he should establish and maintain effective procedures for the validation, storage, protection and maintenance of such products.

Training

* The supplier must identify training needs and provide appropriate training facilities and opportunities.
* Records of training activities should be maintained.

SEVEN

QUALITY IMPROVEMENT TOOLS

◆ INTRODUCTION

As repeatedly indicated earlier, quality improvement starts at the process level. The final product is simply a sum total of several processes spread over the life cycle of the product. To expect to achieve higher levels of product quality, therefore, requires continuous monitoring, control and improvement of the processes. The basic sequence of steps for a typical process improvement program involves the following:

- Identify the process for improvement.
- Identify process characteristics and boundaries.
- Evaluate the current state of control and capability of the process vis-à-vis the specified requirements.
- Challenge the existing assumptions and accepted procedures.
- Identify improvement opportunities.
- Flow chart the process.
- Implement new procedures and initiatives.
- Gather and analyze data through statistical methods.
- Monitor and control the process.
- Analyze problems.
- Eliminate deficiencies and implement improvements.
- Re-evaluate and redefine the new process.
- Assess the performance and identify the improvement achieved.
- Repeat the cycle of continuous improvement.

Process improvement comes through a continuous evaluation of the process performance. There are several excellent analytical tools available for problem identification/analysis and process improvement. These were identified in Chapter 2 and are presented here in Table 10. Some of these tools have been popularly categorized into two groups as follows:

7 Traditional Tools	7 New Tools
• Cause-Effect Diagram	• Relations Diagram
• Pareto Chart	• Affinity Diagram/KJ Method
• Checksheet	• Systematic/Tree Diagram
• Histogram	• Matrix Diagram
• Scatter Diagram	• Matrix Data-Analysis Method
• Control Chart	• Process Decision Program Chart (PDPC)
• Flow Chart	• Arrow Diagram

Both sets of tools are equally and effectively used for various aspects of process improvement. As an example, Table 11 presents a schematic of the sequence of steps for process improvement with an appropriate application of some of the traditional tools. The emergence of new tools is in consequence of the more recent expanded focus on total quality management. In this chapter, we shall only provide a brief description of some of these tools. For a more extensive application of these techniques, the reader is advised to consult other useful sources and references.

◆ BRAINSTORMING

Brainstorming is a process designed to generate ideas from the collective knowledge of a group of people. It is a problem-solving technique used to expand one's thinking to include all the dimensions of a particular topic at hand. The method can be used for:

- Identifying process problems.
- Identifying causes of process problems.
- Generating process improvement ideas.
- Generating improvement implementation ideas.

Table 10. Quality Improvement Tools

Tools and Methodologies	Quality Improvement Activities		
	Problem Identification	Problem Analysis	Planning and Implementation
Brainstorming	✓		✓
Flow Chart	✓		✓
Checksheet	✓		
Histogram	✓		
Cause-Effect Diagram	✓	✓	✓
Pareto Chart	✓	✓	✓
Trend Chart	✓		
Scatter Diagram	✓		
Quality Function Deployment	✓	✓	✓
Force Field Analysis		✓	✓
Shewhart-Deming Cycle		✓	✓
Nominal Group Technique	✓		✓
Benchmarking	✓		✓
Block Diagram	✓	✓	✓
Relations Diagram	✓	✓	
Control Charts	✓	✓	✓
Statistical Process Control	✓	✓	✓
Design of Experiments		✓	
Systematic/Tree Diagram	✓		✓
Arrow Diagram		✓	✓
Affinity Diagram/KJ Method	✓		✓
Matrix Diagram	✓		✓
Matrix Data - Analysis		✓	
Process Decision Program Chart (PDPC)	✓	✓	✓
Concurrent Engineering	✓		✓

Table 11. Process Improvement Steps

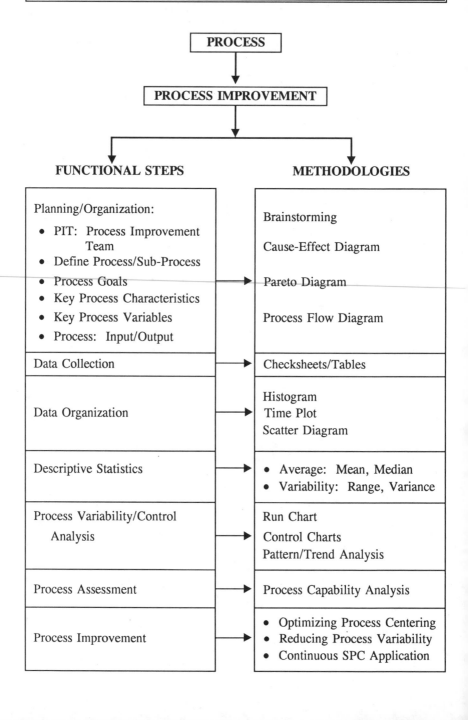

PROCESS

PROCESS IMPROVEMENT

FUNCTIONAL STEPS	METHODOLOGIES
Planning/Organization: • PIT: Process Improvement Team • Define Process/Sub-Process • Process Goals • Key Process Characteristics • Key Process Variables • Process: Input/Output	Brainstorming Cause-Effect Diagram Pareto Diagram Process Flow Diagram
Data Collection	Checksheets/Tables
Data Organization	Histogram Time Plot Scatter Diagram
Descriptive Statistics	• Average: Mean, Median • Variability: Range, Variance
Process Variability/Control Analysis	Run Chart Control Charts Pattern/Trend Analysis
Process Assessment	Process Capability Analysis
Process Improvement	• Optimizing Process Centering • Reducing Process Variability • Continuous SPC Application

The brainstorming process can be structured or unstructured in design. In the structured approach, each person in the group shares an idea as his/her turn comes around or passes until the next turn. The process continues until all the members have run out of ideas. This method facilitates effective participation by everyone involved. The unstructured brainstorming process allows the group members to express their ideas as they come to mind. Although this tends to create a more relaxed setting, it also runs the risk of the session being dominated by the most vocal participants in the group.

Procedure

- Clearly identify the problem on a flip chart.
- State the purpose and objective.
- Each person takes a turn, in sequence, to offer a single idea at a time.
- Record ideas on the flip chart exactly as they are reported.
- Do not interrupt, censor or criticize ideas. Allow for a free and creative flow of thoughts and ideas.
- Do not discuss ideas; questions may be asked for clarification of an idea.
- Encourage participation.
- No individual person should be judged as an expert.
- All ideas are acceptable.
- Ideas can evolve from other people's ideas.
- Allow members to pass when it is their turn but yet contribute further ideas on future turns.
- When everyone passes on a complete turn, the brainstorming session ceases and the list of ideas is turned over to the problem-solving team.

◆ CHECKSHEET

Checksheets are tools that help to collect information and data in an easy and systematic format for compilation and analysis. To effectively use the checksheet, it is important to have a clear understanding of the purpose of data collection and the final results which may be gained from it. Checksheets are generally useful in identifying the:

- Location of defects or parts
- Performance of operations in a sequence
- Reasons for noncompliance
- Process distribution and behaviour
- Defect causes and maintenance checks

Procedure

- Identify the data to be collected.
- Design a checksheet to compile this data.
- Collect the data.
- Tabulate the results.

Table 12 provides an example of a checksheet monitoring various types of defects.

Table 12. Checksheet for Types of Defects		
Process _____ Date _____		
Specification _____ Operator _____		
Defect Type	Tally	Frequency
Crack	### ### ### ### ### //	27
Pinhole	### ### ///	13
Cold Lap	### /	6
Surface Finish	////	4
Miscellaneous	### ###	10
Total		60

♦ QUALITY FUNCTION DEPLOYMENT (QFD)

As defined by Professor Yoji Akado of Japan, Quality Function Deployment means "converting the consumer's requirements into substitute characteristics and setting the designed quality of the finished products by deploying the relationships systematically, starting with the quality of each functional component to the quality of each part and process." Basically, QFD is a means of obtaining a clear understanding of the customer's requirements, translating them into quantitative engineering terms and working together through cross-functional teams, from marketing, design, manufacture and procurement, to meet the customer's needs and requirements. The idea is to incorporate directly into the design of the product the engineering characteristics that match the customer's wants (attributes) and priorities. By doing so, the company can:

- Reduce product introduction time, engineering changes and overall costs.
- Improve cross-functional planning and communication.
- Improve quality, reliability and customer satisfaction.

Procedure

- Establish a well-trained and knowledgeable cross-functional team.
- The team must clearly understand the:
  - Required quality by the customer
  - Designed quality by the management
  - Offered quality by the staff
- Gather complete data/information on the customer requirements.
- Prepare a QFD matrix chart consisting of the:
  - Required quality elements
  - Deployment of quality elements
  - Function deployment
  - Unit parts deployment
  - Technical deployment
  - Deployment with regard to cost and reliability considerations
- The QFD matrix is used to develop an optimal product design that accommodates the customer's priorities and requirements, market needs, product/process alternatives, and available technologies.

♦ FORCE FIELD ANALYSIS

Force Field Analysis is a technique for identifying problems, their causes and the driving forces that help or obstruct a change which affects process improvement. In every situation requiring change or improvement, there is a conjunction of forces which help as well as hinder the process. By identifying both types of forces, an overall strategy can be developed to tackle the change.

Procedure

- Identify the problem.
- Establish a Process Improvement Team.
- Perform a Cause and Effect Analysis.
- Identify all the forces; classify the positive and negative forces separately.
- Prepare the Force Field Diagram (see Figure 1 for example).
- Evaluate the forces with respect to "ease of change" and "impact" on the process.
- Perform a Force Field Analysis:
  - The "restraining forces" are those keeping the problem at its current level (the cause of the problem).
  - The "driving forces" are those pushing the problem toward improvement (the solution to the problem).
- The team develops a strategy to minimize or eliminate the restraining forces and augment the effect of the driving forces to achieve process improvement.

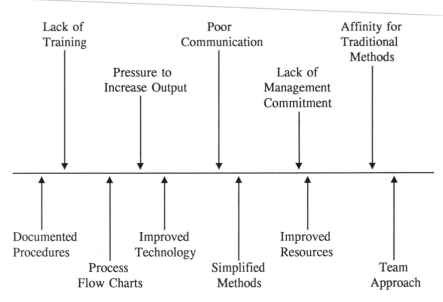

Restraining Forces

Driving Forces

Figure 1: Force Field Analysis for Implementing a Process Change

◆ SHEWHART - DEMING CYCLE

PDSA: Plan-Do-Study-Act

The Shewhart-Deming cycle is a cyclic process for continuous quality improvement. The method is most effective for planning and testing improvement activities prior to full-scale implementation.

Procedure

- Identify opportunities for improvement.
- Identify improvement initiatives.
- Plan and develop a theory to be tested.
- Carry out the trial.
- Collect all relevant data.
- Statistically analyze the results.
- Compare the results with the theory.
- Implement improvement.
- Revise the theory commensurate with this additional knowledge.
- Identify new opportunities for improvement.
- Repeat the continuous improvement cycle.

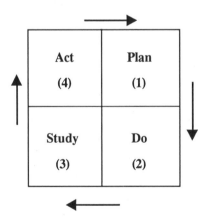

◆ NOMINAL GROUP TECHNIQUE

The Nominal Group Technique is a problem-solving method that involves identifying a problem, developing possible solutions, rank ordering the priorities and selecting the most optimal solution through group consensus.

Procedure

- Identify the problem.
- Gather a team.
- Limit the discussion to one topic per meeting.
- Generate ideas in writing.
- Record ideas without discussion or comments.
- Conduct group discussion to clarify the ideas.
- Do not allow argumentation or criticism of ideas.
- Vote on the results of the discussion.
- Discuss and clarify the vote.
- Establish a final consensus.
- Identify the solution.
- Implement the solution.

◆ BENCHMARKING

Benchmarking is a process in which companies improve their products and services by targeting against and adopting industry's best practices. Whenever a company decides to implement a quality improvement system, it has two options: to reinvent the wheel and develop its own system or to adopt, with or without modification, a system used by another company which has achieved excellence in that area. The latter option is generally more viable, more effective, simpler, less demanding and cost-effective.

Procedure

- Identify the process to be benchmarked.
- Establish a Process Improvement Team.
- Understand the process characteristics and boundaries.
- Identify which companies to benchmark, ie. those with an excellent track record in the area of processes similar to yours or different from yours.
- Establish a relationship with the company and collect and share information.
- Identify the benchmarks by collecting data through surveys, interviews, professional contacts, journals, advertisements, etc.
- Analyze the benchmark data and information.
- Implement and monitor improvement initiatives.
- Evaluate the process performance.
- Continue the cycle of improvement.

◆ STATISTICAL PROCESS CONTROL (SPC)

Statistical Process Control (SPC) is a technique employed to control by means of statistical methods the system of causes and their variability in a process. The basic quality factors of interest in a process are accuracy, precision, bias, process stability, process conformance, uniformity, repeatability and reproducibility. The fundamental characteristic to be controlled is the variability in the process. Variability comes from several sources, such as man, machine, material, method, measurement, money and management. Variability in the process can be measured, evaluated and controlled. To do this, data is collected at critical control points for each process and analyzed through statistical methods. The analysis indicates whether the process is under control or requires a corrective/preventive action. This continuous analysis of on-line process control data helps diagnose and correct problems which otherwise would go unnoticed and become part and parcel of the final product. A product which is well controlled during the process stages with SPC methods will require minimal final inspection and verification.

Procedure

- Identify the process.
- Establish a Process Improvement Team (PIT).
- Establish goals.
- Develop a process flow chart.
- Identify the process inputs and outputs.
- Identify the key process characteristics.
- Brainstorm and prioritize the process characteristics.
- Identify the key process variables.
- Collect process data.
- Analyze process variability.
- Take corrective action.
- Bring the process under statistical control.
- Study the process capability.
- Improve the process through proper experimental design.
- Continue SPC analysis for ongoing improvement.

◆ AFFINITY DIAGRAM/KJ METHOD

The affinity diagram of the KJ (Kawakita Jiro) method is another brainstorming tool to gather ideas, facts and opinions about an unexplored area and organize them into interrelated subgroupings having mutual affinity. This method is most useful in situations where the problem is magnanimous and complex while a simple implementable solution is required. The KJ method stimulates creativity and ensures full team participation.

Procedure

- Identify the problem and state the issue.
- Collect narrative data and record individual responses on small cards.
- Mix the cards and spread them randomly on a large table.
- Sort and group the cards that seem to have mutual affinity. Avoid having too many groups as much as possible.
- Specify a header card that captures the essence of the grouping and place it on top for each group of cards.
- Transfer the information from the cards onto paper with lines surrounding the groupings most closely related.
- The information obtained from this brainstorming exercise helps to identify and highlight improvement opportunities and initiatives.

◆ SYSTEMATIC/TREE DIAGRAM

A tree diagram provides a systematic approach in developing the most appropriate and effective means of accomplishing a given set of objectives. A typical application of a systematic diagram involves:

- Identifying the causes of a problem.
- Refining continuous improvement strategies to achieve excellence.
- Developing objectivity for goals and actions.
- Developing and improving the quality of design for new products.

The systematic diagram is typically an "objective-means" diagram. For each objective, various possible means for achieving it are developed and itemized. The means are then evaluated and prioritized and the objectives are confirmed.

Procedure

- State the objective or goal.
- Generate all possible means or causes.
- Continue the tree diagram by generating further causes or means until all ideas are exhausted.
- Systematize the causes or means.
- Review and confirm the objective.

Figure 2 displays a tree diagram for producing a quality manual.

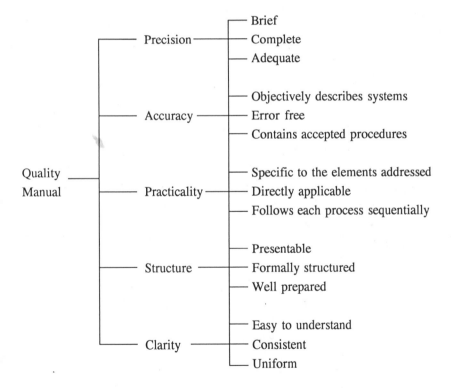

Figure 2: Systematic/Tree Diagram for Producing a Quality Manual

◆ CONCURRENT ENGINEERING (CE)

The traditional approach to design development entailed having individuals or groups in each engineering speciality area work on the design in isolation. Today products have a much higher level of design complexity and sophistication which requires an effective and timely contribution from all responsible participants in the product life cycle to collectively evolve a suitable design.

Concurrent Engineering is the process of developing a viable, suitable and effective design in an optimal time frame through the collective effort of several interrelated cross-functional units. The process necessitates the concurrent application of various engineering specialities and expertise to produce an appropriate design without "stopover" delays. The key elements of a CE process are as follows:

- Total cultural and management transformation from the traditional approach to the new teamwork approach
- Multi-discipline teamwork
- Integrated multi-functional participation
- Disciplined methodology
- Continuous inter and intra-functional interface and communication
- Effective problem-solving and conflict resolution
- Continuous development and improvement of design to satisfy customer requirements and expectations
- Optimization of product/process design, support systems, resources and time constraints

Procedure

- Identify and develop a comprehensive understanding of the customer's requirements and priorities.
- Establish multi-functional teams.
- Identify the total elements and requirements of the product's life cycle.
- Develop an optimal design.
- Test the design.
- Measure performance.
- Institute improvement initiatives.
- Continuously improve the design.

EIGHT

QUALITY SYSTEM ACCREDITATION

◆ DEMONSTRATION OF QUALITY ACHIEVEMENT

When a company has successfully implemented a TQM System and achieved a certain level of quality, it would like to seek means of announcing their achievement. This recognition allows the company:

- To demonstrate their ability to provide high quality products and services.
- To assure their present and prospective customers of their continued commitment to quality.
- To achieve market reputation and credibility.
- To realize expanded and continued market share.

Some of the many ways of achieving recognition include:

- Certification/registration to the ISO-9000 series
- Achieving and meeting the requirements of one of the quality awards, such as the:
  - Malcolm Baldrige National Quality Award
  - Deming Prize for Quality
  - George M. Low Trophy: NASA's Quality and Excellence Award
  - Canada Award for Business Excellence
  - Shingo Prize for Excellence in Manufacturing

Certification to ISO-9000 means that a company's total quality system has been assessed by an independent, third-party accredited certifying organization, known as the Registrar, and found to meet the applicable requirements of the chosen level/quality system standard from the ISO-9000 series. Similarly, qualification to any of the other quality awards is also achieved by meeting the requisite evaluation criteria established for this award.

In as much as there are subtle differences in the approach, focus and emphasis of these quality accreditation processes, there are some fundamental commonalities, such as the following, required by all of these awards:

- Establishment, implementation and maintenance of a total quality management program
- Objective evidence of quality policy, systems, procedures and processes physically and functionally operating in the company
- Evidence of maintenance and continuous quality improvement efforts and results
- Customer satisfaction and delight

The generic procedural steps for accreditation to these awards are as follows:

- Establish, implement and maintain an effective TQM System.
- Select the appropriate award for accreditation consideration.
- Prepare the requisite quality system documentation addressing all the requirements and evaluation criteria of the selected award, eg. quality manual, procedures manuals, work instructions and suitable forms, records, books and files.
- Make an application for third-party accreditation.
- Complete the total audit/assessment process with the accreditor and meet all the requisite requirements.
- Achieve accreditation and maintain/improve the quality status.

The details regarding the process of certification to the ISO-9000 series of quality system standards are covered extensively in Part II of this book. As for the other quality system accreditation awards already mentioned, only a brief outline with its requisite evaluation criteria elements are presented here. For more extensive details, the reader is advised to contact the organization administering the specific award.

This chapter is included only to provide a collective and comprehensive package of information for a comparative evaluation of quality system requirements across various quality accreditation programs. It has been noticed from experience that many companies, while seeking or preparing for accreditation to some program or award, would also like to be aware of other similar accreditation programs and their requisite criteria. This chapter will therefore, prove useful in providing:

- An awareness of various quality accreditation programs and awards
- A comparative evaluation of the quality system requirements for these various awards
- An additional source of information for augmenting the development/implementation of a self-directed TQM System.

◆ MALCOLM BALDRIGE NATIONAL QUALITY AWARD

This award is granted annually to U.S. companies who excel in quality achievement and quality management. There are three eligibility categories for the award: manufacturing companies, service companies and small businesses. Generally, up to two awards are given in each category per year.

To receive the Baldrige Award, a company has to establish a total quality management system and satisfy the evaluation criteria dictated by the award. As a specific example, Table 13 lists the 1991 examination categories/items for the Baldrige Award.

The Malcolm Baldrige Award is managed by the National Institute of Standards and Technology (NIST) and administered by the American Society for Quality Control (ASQC). Further details regarding this award can be obtained from the following:

- United States Department of Commerce
  National Institute of Standards and Technology
  Route 270 and Quince Orchard Road
  Administration Building, Room A537
  Gaithersburg, MD 20899, U.S.A.
  Telephone: (301) 975-2036
  Telefax: (301) 948-3716

Table 13. Malcolm Baldrige National Quality Award

EVALUATION CRITERIA ELEMENTS (1991)

1.0 Leadership

1.1   Senior Executive Leadership
1.2   Quality Values
1.3   Management for Quality
1.4   Public Responsibility

2.0 Information and Analysis

2.1   Scope and Management of Quality Data and Information
2.2   Competitive Comparisons and Benchmarks
2.3   Analysis of Quality Data and Information

3.0 Strategic Quality Planning

3.1   Strategic Quality Planning Process
3.2   Quality Goals and Plans

4.0 Human Resource Utilization

4.1   Human Resource Management
4.2   Employee Involvement
4.3   Quality Education and Training
4.4   Employee Recognition and Performance Measurement
4.5   Employee Well-Being and Morale

5.0 Quality Assurance of Products and Services

5.1   Design and Introduction of Quality Products and Services
5.2   Process Quality Control
5.3   Continuous Improvement of Processes
5.4   Quality Assessment
5.5   Documentation
5.6   Business Process and Support Service Quality
5.7   Supplier Quality

6.0 Quality Results

6.1   Product and Service Quality Results
6.2   Business Process, Operational and Support Service Quality Results
6.3   Supplier Quality Results

7.0 Customer Satisfaction

7.1   Determining Customer Requirements and Expectations
7.2   Customer Relationship Management
7.3   Customer Service Standards
7.4   Commitment to Customers
7.5   Complaint Resolution for Quality Improvement
7.6   Determining Customer Satisfaction
7.7   Customer Satisfaction Results
7.8   Customer Satisfaction Comparison

- American Society for Quality Control
  611 East Wisconsin Avenue
  P.O. Box 3005
  Milwaukee, WI 53202-3005, U.S.A.
  Telephone: (414) 272-8575
  Telefax: (414) 272-1734

◆ THE DEMING PRIZE FOR QUALITY

The Deming Prize was instituted in 1951 by the Union of Japanese Scientists and Engineers (JUSE) in recognition of Dr. Deming's contributions to the quality improvement and achievement efforts in Japan. There are three different categories for the award: The Deming Prize for Individual Person, the Deming Application Prize, and the Quality Control Award for Factory adjudged by the Deming Prize Committee.

The Deming Application Prize is awarded each year by the Deming Prize Committee to an applicant adjudged meritorious by the committee. Originally, the Deming Prize was restricted to Japanese companies; however, since 1984, it has been extended to allow candidate acceptance of oversea companies.

The evaluation criteria elements for the 1989 Deming Application Prize for Quality are listed in Table 14. Further details regarding the Deming Prize can be obtained from the following:

- Union of Japanese Scientists and Engineers
  5.10-11 Sendagaya
  Shibuya - Ku
  Tokyo 151, Japan
  Telephone: 03-5379-1219
  Telefax: 03-356-1798

Table 14. Deming Application Prize for Quality

EVALUATION CRITERIA ELEMENTS (1989)

1. Policy

   1) Policies pursued for management, quality and quality control
   2) Method of establishing policies
   3) Justifiability and consistency of policies
   4) Utilization of statistical methods
   5) Transmission and diffusion of policies
   6) Review of policies and the results achieved
   7) Relationship between policies and long- and short-term planning

2. Organization and Its Management

   1) Explicitness of the scopes of authority and responsibility
   2) Appropriateness of delegations of authority
   3) Interdivisional cooperation
   4) Committees and their activities
   5) Utilization of staff
   6) Utilization of QC Circle activities
   7) Quality control diagnosis

3. Education and Dissemination

   1) Education programs and results
   2) Quality- and control-consciousness, degrees of understanding of quality control
   3) Teaching of statistical concepts and methods, and the extent of their dissemination
   4) Grasp of the effectiveness of quality control
   5) Education of related company (particularly those in the same group, subcontractors, consignees, and distributors)
   6) QC Circle activities
   7) System of suggesting ways of improvements and its actual conditions

4. Collection, Dissemination and Use of Information on Quality

   1) Collection of external information
   2) Transmission of information between divisions
   3) Speed of information transmission (use of computers)
   4) Data processing, statistical analysis of information and utilization of the results

5. Analysis

   1) Selection of key problems and themes
   2) Propriety of the analytical approach
   3) Utilization of statistical methods
   4) Linkage with proper technology
   5) Quality analysis, process analysis
   6) Utilization of analytical results
   7) Assertiveness of improvement suggestions

Table 14. Deming Application Prize for Quality (continued)

EVALUATION CRITERIA ELEMENTS (1989)

6. Standardization

   1) Systematization of standards
   2) Method of establishing, revising, and abolishing standards
   3) Outcome of the establishment, revision, or abolition of standards
   4) Contents of the standards
   5) Utilization of statistical methods
   6) Accumulation of technology
   7) Utilization of standards

7. Control

   1) Systems for the control of quality and such related matters as cost and quantity
   2) Control items and control points
   3) Utilization of such statistical control methods as control charts and other statistical concepts
   4) Contribution to performance of QC Circle activities
   5) Actual conditions of control activities
   6) State of matters under control

8. Quality Assurance

   1) Procedure for the development of new products and services (analysis and upgrading of quality, checking of design, reliability, and other properties)
   2) Safety and immunity from product liability
   3) Process design, process analysis, and process control and improvement
   4) Process capability
   5) Instrumentation, gauging, testing, and inspecting
   6) Equipment maintenance and control of subcontracting, purchasing, and services
   7) Quality assurance system and its audit
   8) Utilization of statistical methods
   9) Evaluation and audit of quality
   10) Actual state of quality assurance

9. Results

   1) Measurement of results
   2) Substantive results in quality, services, delivery time, cost, profits, safety, environment, etc.
   3) Intangible results
   4) Measures for overcoming defects

10. Planning for the Future

   1) Grasp of the present state of affairs and the concreteness of the plan
   2) Measures for overcoming defects
   3) Plans for further advances
   4) Linkage with long-term plans

◆ GEORGE M. LOW TROPHY: NASA'S QUALITY AND EXCELLENCE AWARD

While all the other quality awards are open to any manufacturing company, the George M. Low Trophy is awarded only to NASA's current or prospective contractors, subcontractors and suppliers in the aerospace industry. The award is a recognition of those companies who have demonstrated sustained excellence and outstanding achievements in quality and productivity for three or more years. The award program is managed by the NASA Quality and Productivity Improvement Programs Division and is jointly administered by NASA and the American Society for Quality Control (ASQC).

The general evaluation criteria elements for the 1992 George M. Low Trophy are appended in Table 15. For additional details, contact the ASQC (address given above) or NASA's office as follows:

- NASA Quality and Productivity Improvement Programs Division
  NASA Headquarters - Code QB
  Washington, DC 20546, U.S.A.
  Telephone: (202) 453-8415
  Telefax: (202) 426-1729

◆ CANADA AWARD FOR BUSINESS EXCELLENCE

This award was created in 1984 by the Government of Canada to honour businesses in all industry sectors for their outstanding achievements. The award covers achievement in eight categories: entrepreneurship, environment, industrial design, innovation, invention, marketing, quality, and small business.

The award for the "Quality" category is given in recognition of outstanding achievement in overall business quality through a commitment to continuous quality improvement. Emphasis is placed on the total involvement of the company, including all business functions and all employees, on the competitiveness of the products or services in the marketplace and on a high level of customer satisfaction.

The evaluation criteria elements for the "Quality" category of the 1992 Canada Award for Business Excellence are appended in Table 16. Further information on the award can be obtained from the following:

- Canada Award for Business Excellence
  Industry, Science and Technology Canada
  235 Queen Street
  Ottawa, Ontario, Canada K1A 0H5
  Telephone: (613) 954-4079
  Telefax: (613) 954-4074

◆ THE SHINGO PRIZE FOR EXCELLENCE IN MANUFACTURING

Established in 1988, the Shingo Prize for Excellence in Manufacturing promotes world class manufacturing and recognizes American companies and plants which excel in productivity, quality, customer satisfaction, and their manufacturing processes. The Shingo Prize may be awarded to as many as three businesses in each of the two prize categories: large manufacturing companies, subsidiaries or plants and small manufacturing companies.

The evaluation criteria elements for the prize are appended in Table 17. The Shingo Prize is administered by the Office of Business Relations at Utah State University's College of Business. For further information, contact the following:

- The Shingo Prize
  College of Business
  Utah State University
  Logan, UT   84322-3521, U.S.A.
  Telephone: (801) 750-2281
  Telefax: (801) 750-3440

Table 15. George M. Low Trophy: NASA's Quality and Excellence Award

EVALUATION CRITERIA ELEMENTS (1992)

1.0 Performance Achievements

1.1 Customer Satisfaction

1.1.1 Contract performance
1.1.2 Schedule
1.1.3 Cost

1.2 Quality

1.2.1 Quality Assurance (hardware/software/service)
1.2.2 Vendor quality assurance and involvement
1.2.3 External communication
1.2.4 Problem prevention and resolution

1.3 Productivity

1.3.1 Software utilization
1.3.2 Process improvement and equipment modernization
1.3.3 Resources conservation
1.3.4 Effective use of human resources

2.0 Process Achievements

2.1 Commitment and Communication

2.1.1 Top management commitment/involvement
2.1.2 Goals, planning, and measurement
2.1.3 Internal communication

2.2 Human Resource Activities

2.2.1 Training
2.2.2 Work force involvement
2.2.3 Awards and recognition
2.2.4 Health and safety

Table 16. Canada Award for Business Excellence

Category: Total Quality ‿

EVALUATION CRITERIA ELEMENTS (1992)

Business Background

This information is required by the jury, but not weighted. The information should identify the following elements:

- Business Profile
- Industry Comparison
- Company Location
- Organization
- Major customers and suppliers

Quality Improvement Policy and Plan

1.a   Policy and Definitions
1.b   Quality Improvement Plan and Development
1.c   Planned Measurements of Quality

Implementation of Policy and Plan

2.a   Promulgation of Quality Policy
2.b   Leadership, Deployment and Tracking
2.c   Customer Needs and Assurance of These Needs
2.d   Employee Involvement, Coaching and Training
2.e   Innovative Quality Improvement Techniques

Results Achieved

3.a   Product or Service Improvement and Customer Satisfaction
3.b   Further Results and Benefits

Future Planning

4.a   Future Planning for Quality Improvement
4.b   Planning New Products or Services

Table 17. The Shingo Prize for Excellence in Manufacturing

(Utah State University's College of Business)

EVALUATION CRITERIA ELEMENTS

I. **Strategic Leadership, Involvement, and Support**

    A.   Management Leadership

    B.   Employee Involvement

    C.   Business Process, Operations, and Support Service Improvement

II. **Manufacturing Methods, Systems and Processes**

III. **Measured Improvements in Productivity, Quality, and Customer Satisfaction**

    A.   Productivity

    B.   Quality

    C.   Customer Satisfaction

IV. **Summary of Achievements**

V. **Future Vision/Direction**

PART TWO

ISO 9000

CERTIFICATION

NINE

QUALITY SYSTEM STANDARDS

◆ QUALITY AND STANDARDIZATION

Throughout the process of planning, achieving and improving quality, it becomes absolutely necessary to know:

- How much quality is better quality?
- How much more to improve?
- Is there a yardstick to measure the level and extent of quality achieved?
- Is everyone else using the same measuring gage to assess quality?
- How can a comparative evaluation of the quality status of various suppliers be made?
- Can a "common quality denominator" be established?

For an enterprise, this information is vital to strategic planning for continuous improvement, marketability and profitability. For the customer, it affords a measure of assurance, reliability and comparative evaluation. For the regulators, it provides assurance about compliance, consumer protection, market transparency and fair competition.

Standardization provides the most basic and effective answer to these questions. Standardization is defined as: "a process of formulating and applying rules for an orderly approach to a scientific activity." Standardization of quality activities, therefore, helps to:

- Establish a "common denominator" of business quality accepted by everyone.
- Create simplicity out of complexity.
- Harmonize diverse practices.

- Generate compatibility and uniformity in the application of industrial practices.
- Act as a medium of communication of ideas and information between the buyer and the seller.
- Assist in reducing trade barriers.
- Encourage market transparency and fair competition.

♦ QUALITY SYSTEM STANDARDS

Quality system standards are developed by accredited standard-writing organizations at the national as well as the international level. Standards can be developed for specific industry applications or can be generic in nature, having applications across industry lines. There are many international bodies which are engaged in developing standards for specific industry applications, but the activity on the development of quality assurance standards has generally been limited to the national level.

National standards on quality are normally developed under the umbrella of the National Standards System of the country. Most of the industrialized infrastructures have well-established quality standards. For example, some of the well-known national Quality System Standards include:

Canada:	Z-299 series
France:	AFNOR X 50-110
Germany:	DIN 55-355
Netherlands:	NEN 2646
U.K.:	BS-5750 series
U.S.A.:	ANSI/ASQC Z-1.15, C-1; MIL-Q-9858A, etc.
NATO:	AQAP series

Despite the existence of these national standards, there has always been a desire and a need to have a universally accepted, harmonized set of generic quality assurance standards applicable across all industry lines. This gap has been filled by the International Organization for Standardization (ISO) through one of its technical committees, ISO/TC 176: Quality Management and Quality Assurance. This committee, through its deliberations, provided in 1987 a series (known as the ISO-9000 series) of quality system standards. The ISO-9000 series was derived, through the consensus principle, from a number of national standards to provide the industry with guidelines on how to establish a system for managing product quality in a manufacturing situation. Its objective is to promote the development of standards world-wide to improve operating efficiency, productivity and quality.

◆ THE ISO-9000 SERIES

The quality system standards developed thus far by ISO/TC 176 are appended in Table 18.

Table 18. ISO/TC 176: Quality System Standards

ISO-9000 (1987):	Quality Management and Quality Assurance Standards - Guidelines for Selection and Use
ISO-9001 (1987):	Quality Systems - Model for Quality Assurance in Design/Development, Production, Installation and Servicing
ISO-9002 (1987):	Quality Systems - Model for Quality Assurance in Production and Installation
ISO-9003 (1987):	Quality Systems - Model for Quality Assurance in Final Inspection and Test
ISO-9004 (1987):	Quality Management and Quality System Elements - Guidelines
ISO-8402 (1986):	Quality - Vocabulary

In this series, ISO-9000 and ISO-9004 are not standards; they are only advisory in nature, providing guidelines. The ISO-9001, ISO-9002 and ISO-9003 constitute the actual three-level series of (external) quality assurance standards for use in a two-party contractual situation. ISO-8402 provides definitions and terminology used in the ISO-9000 series.

ISO-9000 provides guidelines and a road-map for the selection and use of the appropriate quality system, namely, ISO-9001, 9002, or 9003. Similarly, ISO-9004 provides quality management and quality system element guidelines for any producer organization to develop and implement a quality system and to determine the extent to which each quality system element is applicable.

The three-tier model of the ISO-9000 series represents three distinct forms of functional or organizational capability suitable for two-party contractual purposes. As originally intended, the series was developed to be used as a second-party contractual document between the buyer and seller to assure the buyer that the seller could furnish an acceptable product or service at the stipulated level of quality. However, the role and application of the series has gone beyond its original mandate. For instance, today many organizations are using ISO-9004 as a first-party document to develop and evaluate their own internal quality management system. Also, organizations are seeking third-party accreditation and certification to one of the three quality levels (ISO-9001, 9002, 9003) as a means of demonstrating and assuring, at large, that the company is operating on and committed to meeting the highest standards of quality.

In general, the ISO-9000 series provides a harmonized set of generic quality assurance standards applicable to any manufacturing situation, with or without some requisite modifications. The series can be conveniently used in conjunction with any existing quality assurance or industry specific standard. The ISO-9000 series provides excellent guidelines on how to commence structuring and implementing an effective quality management system. It provides the foundation on which to build a suitable quality improvement system. Notwithstanding however, the series should still be looked upon as a set of minimum quality system requirements - as the lowest common denominator of quality system elements applicable across all industries, technologies and services.

Since the inception of the ISO-9000 series of Quality System Standards, a number of significant developments have been set into motion:

- A base line agreement about a quality system's minimum requirements has been established.
- Conformance to ISO-9000 is becoming a business mandate of the 1990's.

- Companies who have not been previously involved in any serious quality improvement effort are being forced, by increasing competition in both local and international markets, to implement quality management systems and conform to ISO-9000 standards.
- Customers are getting the opportunity to evaluate the quality performance of suppliers, regardless of the product type or location of production.
- The standards have been adopted by most industrialized nations, either as their national standards or along with and parallel to their national standards. Today, forty-nine countries have either adopted the ISO-9000 series standards or have registration services which offer accreditation to these standards, and this number is continuously growing. Some examples include the following:

- U.S.A.

The equivalent standards in the U.S.A. are known as the Q-90 series. Except for some cosmetic changes, the Q-90 series is identical to the ISO-9000 series.

- U.K.

The BS-5750 series of the U.K. is equivalent to the ISO-9000 series.

- European Community (EC) Standards Organizations (CEN/CENELEC)

The EN29000 to EN29004 series of the EC corresponds to the ISO-9000 to ISO-9004 standards.

- Canada

The existing Canadian national standards on quality assurance are a four-tier model: Z-299.1 to Z-299.4. To align these with the 3-tier ISO-9000 standards, Canada has developed the Q-9000 series, accommodating both the Z-299 series and ISO-9000 series. The CAN/CSA - Q-9000-91 will be an adoption of ISO-9000 - 1987. The ISO-9004 has already been adopted as the Canadian National Standard: CAN/CSA-Q420-87. The CAN/CSA - Q-9001, Q-9002, Q-9003 - 1991 are respectively an adoption of ISO-9001, 9002, 9003 - 1987 with supplementary requirements. The supplementary requirements are included to accommodate Z-299.1, 299.2, 299.3 and 299.4.

◆ THE THREE-TIER MODEL: ISO-9001, 9002, 9003

The type of information contained in these three models is as follows:

Model 1: ISO-9001

This model is for use when conformance to specified requirements is to be assured by the supplier throughout the whole cycle from design, production, installation to servicing. It covers organizations such as, engineering and construction firms and manufacturers that design, develop, produce, install, and service products.

Model 2: ISO-9002

A slightly less stringent than ISO-9001 level, this model is for use when conformance to specified requirements are to be assured during production and installation. This level is particularly suited to the process industries (food, chemical, pharmaceutical, etc.) where the specific requirements for the product are stated in terms of an already established design or specification.

Model 3: ISO-9003

This model applies to situations where the supplier's capabilities are to be assured only for final inspection and tests. It is suitable for small shops, divisions within an organization, laboratories, or equipment distributors that inspect and test supplied products.

ISO-9001 consists of twenty required quality system elements (see Table 19). It represents the fullest and most stringent requirements for system elements outlined in ISO-9004 (see Table 20).

ISO-9002 also accommodates nearly all the quality system elements listed in ISO-9004, though some are treated a little less stringently. This model involves eighteen of the twenty system elements of ISO-9001. The two elements that are not part of ISO-9002 are: "Design Control" and "Servicing".

Since ISO-9003 relates only to those elements concerning final inspection and test, it has the least number of requirements of the three models. Table 20 presents a description of the system elements outlined in ISO-9004 and compares the extent to which they are required by ISO-9001, ISO-9002 and ISO-9003 (reproduced from ISO-9000 - Annex).

◆ PREMISE OF THE ISO-9000 SERIES

As indicated earlier, this international standard is not a product specification standard; it is a management system standard. It is concerned with how organizations provide a quality in their products and services to customers consistently all the time.

Most companies have quality control in some shape or form, and they are generally very happy with their system. Although quality control has its virtues and a place in the total quality management system, its scope is limited. The basic purpose of quality control is to verify, after the job is done, that it's been done correctly. This after-the-fact police force action has little proactive emphasis on the elimination of the causes of nonconformity. Also, quality control actions are generally not formally recorded or analyzed to identify why things went wrong and to make sure the same thing does not reoccur.

The ISO-9000 series attempts to address the overall quality management system to improve and maintain the quality of products and services. It recognizes that the total quality process involves all the departments and functions of the organization. Everyone has a role to play in assuring quality. Consequently, it emphasizes a documented disciplined approach in:

- Clearly identifying management policies and commitment.
- Identifying roles, responsibilities and authority.
- Establishing clear set of instructions to all personnel affecting quality.
- Developing precise procedures and instructions in all areas of operational activity to ensure consistency and uniformity.

Table 19. ISO-9001: Quality System Elements

1. Management Responsibility

   • Quality policy
   • Organization
     • Responsibility and authority
     • Verification resources and personnel
     • Management representative
   • Management review

2. Quality System

3. Contract Review

4. Design Control

   • General
   • Design and development planning
     • Activity assignment
     • Organizational and technical interfaces
   • Design input
   • Design output
   • Design verification
   • Design changes

5. Document Control

   • Document approval and issue
   • Document changes/modifications

6. Purchasing

   • General
   • Assessment of sub-contractors
   • Purchasing data
   • Verification of purchased product

7. Purchaser Supplied Product

8. Product Identification and Traceability

9. Process Control

   • General
   • Special processes

10. Inspection and Testing

    • Receiving inspection and testing
    • In-process inspection and testing
    • Final inspection and testing
    • Inspection and test records

11. Inspection, Measuring and Test Equipment

12. Inspection and Test Status

13. Control of Nonconforming Product

    • Nonconformity review and disposition

14. Corrective Action

15. Handling, Storage, Packaging and Delivery

    • General
    • Handling
    • Storage
    • Packaging
    • Delivery

16. Quality Records

17. Internal Quality Audits

18. Training

19. Servicing

20. Statistical Techniques

Table 20. International Quality Standards: ISO-9000 Series Cross-reference List of Quality System Elements

Clause (or sub-clause) No. in ISO-9004	Title	Corresponding clause (or sub-clause) No. in		
		ISO-9001	ISO-9002	ISO-9003
4	Management responsibility	4.1 ●	4.1 ○	4.1 □
5	Quality system principles	4.2 ●	4.2 ●	4.2 ○
5.4	Auditing the quality system (internal)	4.17 ●	4.16 ○	---
6	Economics - Quality-related cost considerations	---	---	---
7	Quality in marketing (Contract review)	4.3 ●	4.3 ●	---
8	Quality in specification & design (Design control)	4.4 ●	---	---
9	Quality in procurement (Purchasing)	4.6 ●	4.5 ●	---
10	Quality in production (Process control)	4.9 ●	4.8 ●	---
11	Control of production	4.9 ●	4.8 ●	---
11.2	Material control & traceability (Product identification & traceability)	4.8 ●	4.7 ●	4.4 ○
11.7	Control of verification status (Inspection & test status)	4.12 ●	4.11 ●	4.7 ○
12	Product verification (Inspection & testing)	4.10 ●	4.9 ●	4.5 ○
13	Control of measuring & test equipment (Inspection, measuring & test equipment)	4.11 ●	4.10 ●	4.6 ○
14	Nonconformity (Control of nonconforming product)	4.13 ●	4.12 ●	4.8 ○
15	Corrective action	4.14 ●	4.13 ●	---
16	Handling & post-production functions (Handling, storage, packaging & delivery)	4.15 ●	4.14 ●	4.9 ○
16.2	After-sales service	4.19 ●	---	---
17	Quality documentation & records (Document control)	4.5 ●	4.4 ●	4.3 ○
17.3	Quality records	4.16 ●	4.15 ●	4.10 ○
18	Personnel (Training)	4.18 ●	4.17 ○	4.11 □
19	Product safety & liability	---	---	---
20	Use of statistical methods (Statistical techniques)	4.20 ●	4.18 ●	4.12 ○
---	Purchaser supplied product	4.7 ●	4.6 ●	---

KEY
● Full requirement   □ Less stringent than ISO-9002
○ Less stringent than ISO-9001   --- Element not present

NOTES
1. The clause (or sub-clause) titles quoted in the table above have been taken from ISO-9004; the titles given in parentheses have been taken from the corresponding clauses and sub-clauses in ISO-9001, ISO-9002 and ISO-9003.
2. Attention is drawn to the fact that the quality system element requirements in ISO-9001, ISO-9002 and ISO-9003 are in many cases, but not in every case, identical.

Thus, by shifting the focus of quality from the traditional approaches of quality control and quality assurance to management control and process improvement, the standard ensures the production of the right quality the first time. However, by doing so, the standard indeed does not profess to deal with only the highest possible level of product quality. It is quite sensitive to commercial reality in the market place and does not seek to impose levels of quality which are unrealistic, unnecessary or commercially nonviable. It equates "quality" to "fitness for purpose" and the quality system standards as the basic framework for the application of common sense principles to achieve operational consistency.

◆ QUALITY STANDARDS - FUTURE DEVELOPMENTS

As part of their mandate, the ISO/TC 176 has the continual responsibility to:

- Develop other relevant and supporting standards.
- Undertake the five-yearly review of standards.

The ISO-9000 series, which was established in 1987, will be due for its first revision in 1992. It is anticipated that the 1992 revision would not entail any extensive change in the current content and format of the series. However, the 1997 revision would perhaps accommodate the various needs and requirements that will emerge over this period of time and reflect these changes in the series.

At present, ISO/TC 176 has developed the following additional quality related standards that should become available in the near future.

- ISO-9000: Quality Management and Quality Assurance Standards

    - Part 2: Guide for the Implementation of ISO-9001, ISO-9002, ISO-9003
    - Part 3: Guidelines for the Application of ISO-9001 to the Development, Supply and Maintenance of Software.

- ISO-9004: Quality Management and Quality System Elements

    - Part 2: Guidelines for Services
    - Part 4: Guidelines for Quality Improvement

- ISO-8402-1: Quality Concepts and Terminology

    - Part 1: Generic Terms and Definitions

- ISO-10011: Guidelines for Auditing Quality Systems

    - Part 1: Auditing
    - Part 2: Qualification Criteria for Quality System Auditors
    - Part 3: Management of Audit Programs

Table 21 presents a schematic of the ISO family of current and anticipated quality system standards being developed by ISO/TC 176.

◆ OTHER QUALITY RELATED STANDARDS/GUIDES

It is almost imperative for every company implementing a TQM system or ISO-9000 certification to understand that process management and improvement is fundamental to an effective TQM or ISO-9000 implementation and maintenance. Process improvement is accomplished through the use of statistical process control (SPC) methods, such as Pareto diagrams, cause-effect diagrams, control charts, sampling methods, quality function deployment techniques, etc.

The ISO technical committee, TC/69: Applications of Statistical Methods, carries out this task of developing standards and guides on tools and methodologies that provide process control and analytical support to quality system standards such as the ISO-9000 series. Some of the important contributions of this committee are appended in Table 22.

Table 21. ISO Family of Quality System Standards (Current and Anticipated)

THE QUALITY SYSTEM STANDARDS		
ISO-9001	ISO-9002	ISO-9003

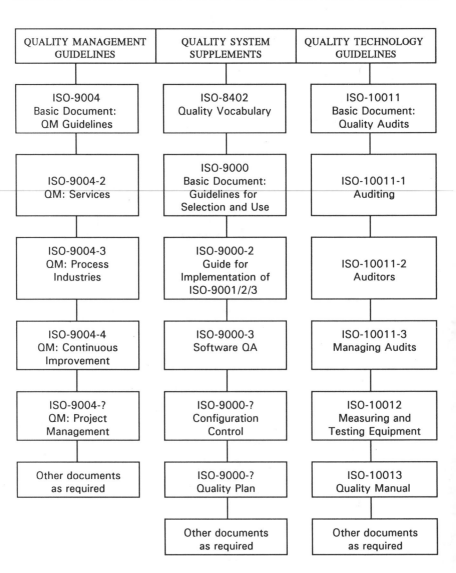

QUALITY MANAGEMENT GUIDELINES	QUALITY SYSTEM SUPPLEMENTS	QUALITY TECHNOLOGY GUIDELINES
ISO-9004 Basic Document: QM Guidelines	ISO-8402 Quality Vocabulary	ISO-10011 Basic Document: Quality Audits
ISO-9004-2 QM: Services	ISO-9000 Basic Document: Guidelines for Selection and Use	ISO-10011-1 Auditing
ISO-9004-3 QM: Process Industries	ISO-9000-2 Guide for Implementation of ISO-9001/2/3	ISO-10011-2 Auditors
ISO-9004-4 QM: Continuous Improvement	ISO-9000-3 Software QA	ISO-10011-3 Managing Audits
ISO-9004-? QM: Project Management	ISO-9000-? Configuration Control	ISO-10012 Measuring and Testing Equipment
Other documents as required	ISO-9000-? Quality Plan	ISO-10013 Quality Manual
	Other documents as required	Other documents as required

Table 22. ISO/TC 69: Quality Related Standards

ISO-3534: Statistics-Vocabulary and Symbols

- Part 1: Probability and General Statistical Terms
- Part 2: Statistical Quality Control
- Part 3: Design of Experiments

ISO-2859: Sampling Inspection Procedures for Inspection by Attributes

- Part 0: Introduction to ISO-2859
- Part 1: Sampling Plans Indexed by Acceptable Quality Level (AQL) for Lot-by-Lot Inspection
- Part 2: Sampling Plans Indexed by Limiting Quality (LQ) for Isolated Lot Inspection
- Part 3: Skip Lot Sampling Plan

ISO-3951: Sampling Procedures and Charts for Inspection by Variables for Percent Nonconforming

ISO-7870: General Guide and Introduction to Control Charts

ISO-8258: Shewhart Control Charts

ISO-7966: Acceptance Control Charts

ISO-5725: Accuracy (Trueness and Precision) of Measurement Methods and Results (six parts)

ISO-8550: Guide for Selection of an Acceptance Sampling System Scheme or Plan

ISO-8422: Sequential Sampling Plans for Inspection by Attributes

ISO-8423: Sequential Sampling Plans for Inspection by Variables for Percent Nonconforming (Known Standard Deviation)

Under Preparation

- Process Capability and Performance Measures
- Introduction to Cumulative Sum Charts
- Implementation of Statistical Process Control
- Statistical Aspects of Sampling from Bulk Material
- Acceptance Sampling Plans for Bulk Material
- Applications of Statistical Methods in Standardization and Specifications

In addition, the ISO (International Organization for Standardization) and its sister organization, the IEC (International Electrotechnical Commission), both headquartered in Geneva, have produced some other useful guides pertinent to quality system accreditation and certification. A selected list is appended in Table 23. A majority of these guides relate to either laboratory accreditation work or accredited registration bodies.

These guides do not provide any direct information for ISO-9000 certification; they are listed here only as a useful secondary source of information.

◆ AVAILABILITY OF STANDARDS

Copies of the standards can be purchased either from a national standards body within a country or directly from the central secretariat of the ISO. Some of the corresponding addresses are as follows:

- ISO Office

  International Organization for Standardization
  Central Secretariat
  1, rue de varembé
  Case Postale 56
  CH-1211 Genève 20, Switzerland
  Telephone: +41 22 749 01 11
  Telefax: +41 22 733 34 30

- U.S.A.

  American National Standards Institute
  1430 Broadway
  New York, N.Y. 10018
  Telephone: (212) 354-3300
  Telefax: (212) 302-1286

  American Society for Quality Control
  611 East Wisconsin Avenue
  P.O. Box 3005
  Milwaukee, WI 53202-3005
  Telephone: (414) 272-8575
  Telefax: (414) 272-1734

• U.K.

British Standards Institution
2 Park Street
London, England   W1A 2BS
Telephone: +44 1629 90 00
Telefax: +44 1629 05 06

• CANADA

Standards Council of Canada
45 O'Connor Street
Ottawa, Ontario   K1P 6N7
Telephone: (613) 238-3222
Telefax: (613) 995-4564

Note: 1. Copies of the Canadian Q-9000 series can be obtained from:

Canadian Standards Association
178 Rexdale Boulevard
Rexdale, Ontario   M9W 1R3
Telephone: (416) 747-4000
Telefax: (416) 747-2475

2. Quality System Registrars in Canada:

• Quality Management Institute (QMI)
(a division of Canadian Standards Association)
2 Robert Speck Parkway
Suite 800
Mississauga, Ontario   L4Z 1S1
Telephone: (416) 272-3920
Telefax: (416) 272-3942

• Canadian General Standards Board (CGSB)
Ottawa, Ontario   K1A 1G6
Telephone: (819) 956-0400
Telefax: (819) 956-4716

Table 23. ISO/IEC Guides Pertinent to Quality System Accreditation/Certification

ISO/IEC Guide 16 - Code of principles on third-party certification systems and related standards (1978)

ISO/IEC Guide 23 - Methods of indicating conformity with standards for third-party certification systems (1982)

ISO/IEC Guide 25 - General requirements for the technical competence of testing laboratories (2nd ed. 1982)

ISO/IEC Guide 27 - Guidelines for corrective action to be taken by a certification body in the event of misuse of its mark of conformity (1983)

ISO/IEC Guide 28 - General rules for a model third-party certification system for products (1982)

ISO/IEC Guide 38 - General requirements for the acceptance of testing laboratories (1983)

ISO/IEC Guide 39 - General requirements for the acceptance of inspection bodies (2nd ed. 1988)

ISO/IEC Guide 40 - General requirements for the acceptance of certification bodies (1983)

ISO/IEC Guide 42 - Guidelines for a step-by-step approach to an international certification system (1984)

ISO/IEC Guide 44 - General rules for ISO or IEC international third-party certification schemes for products (1985)

ISO/IEC Guide 48 - Guidelines for third-party assessment and registration of a supplier's quality system (1986)

ISO/IEC Guide 49 - Guidelines for development of a quality manual for a testing laboratory (1986)

ISO/IEC Guide 53 - An approach to the utilization of a supplier's quality system in third-party product certification (1988)

ISO/IEC Guide 54 - Testing laboratory accreditation systems - General recommendations for the acceptance of accreditation bodies (1988)

ISO/IEC Guide 55 - Testing laboratory accreditation systems - General recommendations for operation (1988)

TEN

ISO 9000 CERTIFICATION

◆ STANDARDS-DRIVEN MARKETS

As globalization continues and international trading blocks are formed, like the one in Europe, access to international markets will become especially important. The rules of the game on the international playing field seem to be conformance to the ISO-9000 series of quality system standards. There is a standards-driven quality revolution. The market forces are directing companies to seek third-party evidence of conformance to one of the contractual standards in the ISO-9000 series. Quality system accreditation and registration will become one of the basic requirements before a business contract is awarded.

About ninety countries have accepted the ISO-9000 standards. There is a world-wide political and trade policy trend towards quality system registration. A "certificate of registration" acknowledges that the quality system operated by the firm meets specific requirements. The European markets are attempting to put mandated requirements for ISO-9000 certification. Increasingly, it seems that accreditation will become more and more a requirement for international trading.

◆ ISO-9000 CERTIFICATION

Registration/certification to ISO-9000 means that a company's total quality system has been assessed and has been found to meet the applicable requirements of the chosen level of the ISO-9000 standards. There are two types of certification: two-party certification and third-party certification.

Originally, when the standards were developed, they were intended to be used as a second-party contractual document between the buyer and the seller to assure the buyer that the seller can furnish an acceptable product or service at the stipulated level of quality.

Today, however, most organizations are using the series for third-party certification, that is, seeking an independent accreditation of their quality system in general, without any reference to the current or prospective customer(s). Third-party certification is done by independent accredited Registrars who carry out a comprehensive audit of the company's quality system and provide a seal of approval of its effectiveness.

It should be noted that, in a third-party certification, the auditors of the accredited registrar do not audit the quality of the finished product but rather only carry out a comprehensive quality system audit. Consequently, even when a company may achieve third-party ISO-9000 certification and establish a global credibility, it may still have to comply with all the requisite product inspection/verification requirements stipulated in a bilateral two-party contractual agreement between the buyer and the seller.

It must be clearly understood then that the process of certification is not a means to an end. Some companies, due to market-driven pressures, may be tempted to myopically implement only cosmetic systems to simply achieve accreditation/certification status and keep their customers satisfied. Again, having achieved certification status, some companies may also neglect to pursue their emphasis on continuous improvement. The ultimate goal must be continuous improvement of the system as well as the product, with or without the certification.

Basically, the process of third-party certification to the ISO-9000 series of quality system standards involves the following steps:

- Company establishes an effective TQM System.
- Company selects the appropriate level of ISO standard for certification, ie., ISO-9001, ISO-9002 or ISO-9003.
- Company prepares the requisite quality system documentation.

- Company selects a suitable Quality Registrar and makes an application for registration.
- Registrar carries out a preliminary evaluation followed by a comprehensive on-site audit.
- Company receives a certificate of registration.
- Surveillance of the quality system maintenance ensues.

The following two points should be noted about ISO-9000 certification:

- The certification is done on a plant-by-plant basis; that is, a company or corporation may have several plants/facilities in one city or nationally and internationally, but only that particular plant or facility which implements the quality system, applies for certification and meets the specified requirements will be awarded the certification status.
- Once awarded, the certification status is valid for a period of three years. However, throughout this period, the Registrar conducts a monitoring audit function and the company is obliged to provide to the Registrar documentary evidence of the maintenance of the quality level to which it has been accredited as well as copies of any revisions/changes made in the quality manual.

◆ REGISTRATION PROCESS

The process of registration/certification is not complicated but requires careful planning and preparation. The basic steps are as follows:

- Obtain management commitment.
- Establish a steering team.
- Appoint an ISO-9000 coordinator.
- Review the existing quality system to identify:
  - the state and level of the total quality system functionally operating within the company.
  - the structure and format of the company's quality system vis-à-vis the format and guidelines outlined in ISO-9004.
  - the company's state of preparedness.
  - the format of the current internal quality system documentation, ie., the quality manual, procedures manuals, work instructions, etc.
- Select the appropriate level, ie., ISO-9001, ISO-9002 or ISO-9003, for registration.
- Identify what needs to be done to be able to meet the requirements of the selected standard.
- Conduct in-house awareness/training sessions.

- Develop, compile or revise the quality system documentation vis-à-vis the chosen standard.
- Conduct ongoing quality audits.
- Define, develop and implement new/revised quality system procedures and instructions.
- Implement corrective actions.
- Select a suitable Quality Registrar, make an application for registration and submit the quality manual for assessment.
- Implement improvements recommended by the pre-assessment audit, if any.
- Complete the total on-site audit/assessment process with the Registrar and meet all the specified requirements.
- Take requisite action to remove all discrepancies, as per the Registrar's recommendations.
- Obtain certification status.
- Conduct frequent checks and maintain the certification status.

◆ BENEFITS OF ISO-9000 CERTIFICATION

Over and above the numerous advantages of quality system certification inadvertently mentioned throughout this book, some very specific and direct benefits include the following:

Intrinsic

- Improved control of operations
- Improved internal quality system
- Cost containment through reduced rework, scrap, overtime
- Improved efficiency and productivity
- Improved conformance and compliance
- Decreased liability
- Reduction of costly multiple customer audits
- Increased customer confidence and employee morale

Extrinsic

- World-wide recognition and credibility
- Common denominator of business quality around the world
- Access to European and world markets
- Use of certification label as a status symbol
- Qualification to bid on contracts in new markets
- Expanded and continued market share
- Improved partnership with suppliers and customers

◆ SELECTING THE APPROPRIATE QUALITY MODEL

The selection of the appropriate quality model typically depends on what the company does.

Companies whose operations involve the entire cycle of design, development, production, installation, and servicing would normally be seeking certification to the ISO-9001 level. Since ISO-9001 is the most comprehensive model of the three, it is applicable to organizations with a more comprehensive operational scope, especially where a substantial part of the internal activity relates to the technical design and development of specifications for products or services. Although ISO-9001 commonly applies to manufacturing or processing industries, it can be equally applied to a wide range of other organizations, such as construction or even professional consulting services.

Companies who are not involved in any design function but only produce to an already established design or specification would seek certification to the ISO-9002 model. ISO-9002 applies to manufacturing, processing and even service organizations which work to the technical designs and specifications provided by their customers.

Since the ISO-9003 level concerns only itself with requirements relating to final inspection and testing, this model has a rather limited scope. It applies to organizations whose products or services are quite simple in nature and, as such, their quality can be simply assessed by routine testing and inspection.

The numbering in the three-tier model may give the impression that there is some kind of progression among the tiers and hence organizations seeking certification should start for example, with ISO-9003 and move up to ISO-9001 over a period of time or vice versa. It may also give the impression that certification to ISO-9001 is better than certification to ISO-9002 or ISO-9003. The three models are complete in themselves and the company should select the level that best reflects its activities. Moving from one model to another is possible and reasonable but should occur only when the organization has changed in some way or altered the profile of its total activity for certification purposes.

ISO-9001 and ISO-9002 are much alike in their quality system requirements. The ISO-9001 certification requirements involve twenty elements (see Table 3, Chapter 2) whereas those for ISO-9002 involve eighteen of these twenty. The two elements that are part of ISO-9001 but not ISO-9002 are "Design Control" and "Servicing". Experience has indicated that there are many companies who, even though not directly involved in the "Design" function, still keep a close watch on and provide significant input into the design activities of their suppliers. Similarly, the "Servicing" function is almost an integral part of many processing industries. Thus, even when such companies would normally go for ISO-9002 certification, they should include references to the design and servicing aspects of their operations in their quality system documentation.

In much the same way, companies who are heavily involved in the "Design" function would normally choose to go for ISO-9001 certification. However, if these companies attempt to seek ISO-9002 certification just because it may be easier to achieve, it would really indicate a lack of commitment to quality or a lack of confidence in their design capabilities.

♦ QUALITY SYSTEM DOCUMENTATION

A quality system needs to be established, maintained and documented. The system covers the organization, allocation of responsibilities, procedures, processes and resources which would jointly lead to the provision of goods and services in accordance with the quality policy and objectives. Normally, any company who has a well-established quality management system would have the proper requisite documentation for the system. Preparing the quality system documentation for ISO-9000 certification simply amounts to developing or modifying the existing documentation so as to systematically address and accommodate all the requisite system elements of the applicable ISO-9000 standard.

A quality system is normally documented by means of one or several tiers of documents. One such hierarchy is schematically shown in Figure 1.

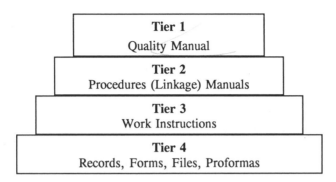

Figure 1: Documentation Hierarchy Pyramid

The first tier documentation consists of the organization's quality assurance manual. It states and defines the management policies, objectives, organizational structure, quality plans, quality system, and review mechanism. Policy dictates what must be done in the organization and provides direction for decision-making. Since the quality manual identifies the overall scope and intent of the system, it must be carefully and thoughtfully prepared. However, the manual should not be large or cumbersome by containing all the procedural details; these should be reserved for the other document levels that are more instructional in nature.

Policy is to be interpreted into procedures that are to be understood and implemented by everyone. The second tier documentation, therefore, constitutes the procedures manuals that list all the quality management core procedures dictated by the policy and used in the organization. They are the linkage of the system elements referenced in the quality manual. The procedures also clarify who does what, in liaison with whom, and under what authority. They cover the whole range of activities, such as contract review, procurement, auditing, process control, inspection and test, nonconformances, training, etc.

Work instructions form the third tier documentation; they are the basic operating instructions identifying how procedures are to be carried out for an effective day-to-day functioning of the system. For instance, they include the standard operating procedures, test methods, calibration methods, detailed specifications for individual products, materials and services, etc. Work instructions are typically the task instructions for specific activities on the shop floor or in the office, such as work schedules, job descriptions, quality cost calculation instructions, plant operating instructions, testing/inspection methods, financial reporting instructions, records of quality control activities, records of quality system audits, safety instructions, etc.

The fourth tier simply consists of all the requisite forms, proformas, books, files and records essential for the documentation and maintenance of the quality system and the effective running of the organization.

This format and structure of the quality system documentation hierarchy as described above should only be viewed as an overall generic documentation framework. By no means should any organization force-fit its operational activities into this framework. For instance, experience has indicated that some small organizations with few procedural details may be able to accommodate their system elements into only one or two levels of documentation: a quality manual and/or a procedural manual containing all their procedures, instructions and proformas. What is important to realize is that the quality documentation should accurately describe the organization's quality policy and operating procedures. Basically, quality system documentation serves the following fundamental purposes:

- They make sure that everyone involved knows what they should be doing, how that should be done and by whom.
- They provide objective evidence to a third-party assessor or to customers that the system is comprehensive and that the organization truly does operate according to the stated management policies and objectives.

◆ CHOOSING A REGISTRAR FOR CERTIFICATION

The certification process is carried out by independent certifying organizations, known as Registrars. Most of the industrialized countries have a host of registrars carrying out the certification task, and this list is growing daily as the demand for certification increases. The difficulty is not finding a registrar, but finding the right one. At the moment, this problem is aggravated by the lack of a well-regulated system for the accreditation of registrars. There is no single, unified, harmonized or internationally accepted system and/or criteria for the certification of registrars. Since any person or company can opt to assume the role of a registrar, the task of finding an appropriate registrar can become somewhat difficult.

Notwithstanding, however, all kinds of efforts are being made to minimize the problem. In the United States of America, the American National Standards Institute (ANSI) and the American Society for Quality Control (ASQC) have jointly established the Registration Accreditation Board (RAB) as the body to formally accredit registrars to carry out quality system certification. In the U.K., the corresponding agency is the National Accreditation Council for Certification Bodies (NACCB). In Europe, the European network for quality system assessment and certification (EQNET) is a network of third-party certification bodies. In Canada, the Standards Council of Canada (SCC) has established the Advisory Committee on Quality (ACQ) to implement a quality registrar accreditation program. Similar registrar accreditation bodies are being formed in other countries as well. Despite this, the following two major issues still remain unresolved:

- There is no universal agreement between these registrar accreditation bodies to recognize each other's accreditation criteria. Any agreement on mutual recognition is still limited to bilateral M.O.U.'s (Memorandum of Understanding), either between the accrediting organizations or between the registrars on a one-to-one basis.
- Although most of the registrar accreditation bodies publish a directory of accredited registrars, the competency of any registrar cannot be judged only on the basis of its registration and accreditation by these accrediting boards. There are indeed many highly competent registrars who have yet chosen not to be registered with these accreditation boards.

In light of the above discussion, companies moving towards ISO-9000 certification are advised to exercise great care in selecting an appropriate registrar. Following are some of the criteria that should be kept in mind:

- Find out if the registrar is recognized by an official government agency or an accreditation board. Check the latest available information about registrars or their accreditation process from the national standardization body, from industrial organizations/associations, or from other reliable sources.
- Investigate range of credibility and recognition that the registrar enjoys - national, international, or both?
- How competent is the registrar? Check his track record of competency and registrations.

- How broad is his range of knowledge and capabilities? Does the registrar possess capabilities in the area of those functions that your company is engaged in? Check the competency/credentials of the auditors used by the registrar.
- What kind of certification procedures and processes are used by the registrar?
- What is the total cost structure for certification by this registrar and how does it compare with that of other registrars?

Following is a partial list of available registrars; some are registered with the accreditation boards while others are not:

- In the U.S.A., some of the registrars are: AT&T'S Quality Registrar, Bureau Veritas Quality International, Quality Management Institute, Det norske Veritas, TUV Rheinland of North America, Lloyd's Register QA, ABS Quality Evaluations, Underwriters Laboratories, Vincotte USA, Quality Systems Registrars, American Gas Association Laboratories, ETL Testing Laboratories, etc. A complete list can be obtained from the Registrar Accreditation Board (RAB):

  - Registrar Accreditation Board (RAB)
    American Society for Quality Control
    611 East Wisconsin Avenue
    P.O. Box 3005
    Milwaukee, WI   53202-3005
    Telephone: (414) 272-8575
    Telefax: (414) 272-1734

- In Canada, there are two registrars the Quality Management Institute (QMI), a division of the Canadian Standards Association (CSA), and the Canadian General Standards Board (CGSB), (addresses on page 23).
- In the U.K., the two well-known registrars are: the Lloyd's Registry and the British Standards Institution (BSI). The BSI (address on page 23) also publishes the Association of Certification Bodies, which lists all certification bodies accredited by the NACCB as well as those not accredited. A list of NACCB accredited registrars can be obtained from:

  - The National Accreditation Council for Certification Bodies (NACCB)
    19 Buckingham Gate
    London, U.K. SWI E6LB
    Telephone: +44 71 233 7111
    Telefax: +44 71 233 5115

ELEVEN

DEVELOPING QUALITY MANUALS

◆ INTRODUCTION

As indicated earlier, for the effective operation of a quality system, its contents must be properly structured and documented. Any company which has a well-established quality management system would normally have the proper requisite documentation for the system, such as the Quality Assurance Manual, the Procedures Manuals and the Work Instructions.

The quality manual is the most important item of the system documentation. It is a silent, but powerful, spokesperson for the company. It clearly identifies, to everyone, the company's commitment to quality through its management mission/vision, quality policy and objectives, systems, procedures and methodologies. This is the document that a company would like to display up front to identify its commitment to quality. It is, therefore, fundamentally important to ensure that the quality manual is developed with utmost tenacity and professionalism.

The procedures manuals and work instructions, on the other hand, are internal to the company and need not be disclosed to anyone except during a mutually consented, requisite quality system audit. These manuals contain operating procedures for the day-to-day functioning of the organization. Although the whole system is dynamic and responsive to the changing conditions, the detailed procedures and area work instructions are the ones most subject to regular revision, often because the organization's position and operating methods keep developing and changing. Therefore, the development of procedures, their review and revision require continuous support from all the personnel and functions impacting quality.

This chapter provides some guidelines for developing a quality manual. The suggested format, structure and contents of the manual are perhaps only one example of the many different ways such a manual can be developed. The manual has to be tailored to the specific needs of the user organization. The ISO/TC 176, technical committee is in the process of developing a standard on "Quality Management: Guidelines for Developing Quality Manuals". Once it is ready and made available, the reader should consult this document for further guidance.

◆ QUALITY MANUAL FUNDAMENTALS

What is a quality manual? The definition given in the committee draft of the international standard ISO/CD 8402-1: "Quality Concepts and Terminology - Part 1: Generic Terms and Definitions" is as follows:

> **"Quality Manual**: A document stating the quality policy and describing the quality system of an organization."

The following "notes" also accompany this definition in the standard:

- A quality manual may relate to the totality of an organization's activities or only to a part of it. The title and scope of the manual reflects the field of application.

- A quality manual will normally contain, or refers to, at least:

  - quality policy

  - the responsibilities, authorities and inter-relationships of personnel who manage, perform, verify or review work affecting quality

  - the quality system procedures and instructions

  - a statement for reviewing, updating and controlling the manual

- A quality manual can vary in depth and format, to suit the needs of an organization. It may be comprised of more than one document. In some instances, when its only purpose is for demonstration, it may be called a "quality assurance manual".

Basically, a quality manual describes the documented quality system procedures intended for the overall planning and administration of activities which impact the quality of an organization's products and services.

The manual generally serves the following purposes:

- It serves as a means of communicating a company's policy, procedures and commitment to quality.
- It formalizes and documents the quality system.
- It assists in the effective implementation and maintenance of the quality system.
- It establishes effective inter and intra-organizational interfaces.
- It provides an improved control of operations.
- It serves as the basis for auditing quality system performance.
- It provides consistency and uniformity in the application of system procedures.
- It provides an objective evidence that the company is truly operating a quality system as per the stated policies and objectives.

Since manuals are indispensable tools and guidebooks for both inexperienced and expert workers, they must be developed with great care. Manuals are meant to make things easier, not more difficult. Therefore, they should be precise, accurate, and simple to understand. They should not be unnecessarily thick or bulky nor contain confusing or complicated instructions and procedures. Manuals should help the worker in finishing the job quickly and right the first time. If the manual is so complicated or long-winded that a worker has to spend time figuring out the manual itself rather than its outlined procedures in order to do a job, then tasks will go unfinished, machines will simply not work and the workers will become unduly demoralized.

The quality manual should be very precise, accurate and to the point. The quality manual should only contain the management mission, the quality policies, objectives, plans and an overall description of the system elements operating in the company. It should not contain procedural details; they should be left for the procedural manuals and work instructions.

Similarly, the procedures manuals should also be precise and not too bulky. They should not be too complicated to be read by the operating personnel. They are not meant to be glossy ornamental pieces to be put on bookshelves; they are to contain practical methods and procedures described in such a way as to let its users work with speed and accuracy to save time, effort, materials and utilities while at the same time protect the worker and the organization from every conceivable risk and danger. An instructions manual for a certain process or piece of equipment is no different. It should be written with clarity and precision. The operator should not be wasting time deciphering the instructions or be forced to remember unnecessary things.

Following are some guidelines for the development of quality manuals:

- The manual should be simple, clear, precise, practical and specific to the elements addressed. Even when each user may have a different level of education and/or experience, the manual should be understandable by all and easy to follow.
- The format and structure should be well thought out and followed consistently and uniformly throughout the manual.
- The sequence of requirements/procedures/instructions should be in line with the sequence of operations.
- The information should be precise, error free, necessary, pertinent and directly applicable. There is no need to give long explanations and complicated theories. The illustrations, flow diagrams or sketches should be simple and not crowded with details. The definitions, abbreviations and terminology should be correct and uniformly acceptable to all. Remember that the user needs to read the manual, apply it and get the job done properly and efficiently.

♦ QUALITY MANUAL PREPARATION

When a quality manual has to be prepared to document the system elements vis-à-vis ISO-9000 certification from either an existing company quality system documentation or from scratch, any or all of the following recommended procedures may be used:

- Establish a team of competent personnel to coordinate and develop the manual.
- Identify the pertinent standard and study its applicable requirements.
- Identify the existing applicable quality system procedures operating in the company.
- Obtain an up-to-date status of the quality system from each function and activity in the organization.
- Establish the format and structure of the intended manual.
- The team, under its leader, starts the actual writing activity. The team leader may:
  - use the services of an outside consultant, if needed.
  - delegate portions of the manual writing activity to other functional units, as appropriate.
  - continually seek up-to-date information from various functions, as required.
- When the draft of the manual is ready, it should be reviewed by:
  - the steering committee or management to ensure accuracy of the statements relating to management commitment, quality policies and objectives.
  - the various Process Improvement Teams or functions of the organization to ensure completeness and accuracy of the system elements, procedures, processes and methodologies.
  - other essential personnel, as appropriate.
- The ultimate responsibility for ensuring the completeness and accuracy of the manual as well as of its contents and writing style lies with the appointed team.
- Before issuing the manual, the document should be subjected to a final review by the appropriate responsible personnel.
- Finally, procedures must be established for the distribution, control, development, review and revision of the manual.

◆ QUALITY MANUAL: FORMAT AND STRUCTURE

Although there is no required structure or format for the quality manual, the following guidelines should provide sufficient assistance in developing a suitable manual. For the specific purpose of ISO-9000 registration, a quality manual should be prepared, chapter by chapter, responding to all the clauses outlined in the selected ISO standard and identifying clearly and accurately the systems and procedures operating in the company. For the purpose of illustration, the ISO-9001 level is selected as an example to elucidate the method of developing the format, structure and content of a quality manual.

Typically, the manual would include, as a preamble, a series of introductory chapters such as:

- Cover Page
- Table of Contents
- Scope and Applicability
- Ownership Page
- Certification of Quality Manual
- Foreword
- Statement of Authority
- Manual Revision Status
- Definitions and Abbreviations

Next, the manual would address, clause by clause, all the system elements of ISO-9001 describing the quality system and procedures operating in the company, as follows:

ISO-9001: System Elements

1. Management responsibility
2. Quality system
3. Contract review
4. Design control
5. Document control
6. Purchasing
7. Purchaser supplied product
8. Product identification and traceability
9. Process control
10. Inspection and testing
11. Inspection, measuring and test equipment
12. Inspection and test status
13. Control of nonconforming product
14. Corrective action
15. Handling, storage, packaging and delivery
16. Quality records
17. Internal quality audits
18. Training
19. Servicing
20. Statistical techniques

Preamble of the Quality Manual

- Cover Page: sets out the company's name and location, the title of the quality manual and the level of the standard being addressed.
- Table of Contents: provides a total list of the contents addressed in the manual.
- Scope and Applicability: clearly identifies the scope and applicability of the quality manual.
- Ownership Page: identifies ownership responsibilities, copyright considerations and entitlement for usage.
- Certification of Quality Manual: a certification to the effect that the quality manual adequately and accurately describes the quality system in use within the company. This page must be signed and dated by the President and the Quality Manager.
- Foreword: presents a summary of the overall functions of the manual and includes such items as the level of standard being addressed, the quality management systems and procedures being used by the company to ensure a high conformance and quality level, and any other relevant information essential to highlight the effective functioning of the quality system.
- Statement of Authority: clearly sets out the responsibilities and the authority of the Quality Manager and staff dealing with quality matters. It would be appropriate for this page to be signed and dated by the President of the company.
- Manual Revision Status: a form to identify and list all revisions with corresponding dates and authorization. The revision notice is to be sent to all those who have been issued a copy of the manual.
- Definitions and Abbreviations: provides the relevant definitions and abbreviations used in the manual.

Format and Structure

The format and structure of the manual also require careful consideration. A standardized format can be developed to achieve consistency and uniformity. For instance, the top of each page in the manual should bear the company name and logo (if practical), the title of the ISO-9001 clause being addressed and the document control information, such as the page number, section, issue, total number of pages for the title clause and date.

The description of the system elements for each clause can also be categorized under standardized headings, such as:

- Purpose
- Scope
- Responsibility
- General Procedures
- References

A sample of the suggested format is shown in Table 24.

Table 24. Quality System Manual: Sample Format		
LOGO ABC Company, Inc. Lovers Lane Quality Land	Quality System Manual	Section: D Issue: 1 Page: 1 of 3 Date: 1992 - 07 - 27
DESIGN CONTROL **Purpose** **Scope** **Responsibility** **General Procedures** **References**		

After the introductory chapters of the quality manual have been developed, the manual then addresses, clause by clause, the system elements of ISO-9001. Each clause describes what is required to be included in the Quality System Manual to meet the ISO-9001 requirements vis-à-vis what is being done within the company. One should follow each clause, item by item, and identify all the management systems, procedures and processes operating in the company. To facilitate interpretation of the requirements of each clause, a detailed package of guidelines and an action checklist have been prepared and included in Chapters 8 and 9 respectively.

TWELVE

QUALITY SYSTEM AUDITING

♦ ROLE OF QUALITY AUDITS

Auditing is fundamental to quality assessment and improvement. A quality audit is an objective evaluation of the effectiveness of the quality system. It provides a timely comprehensive status report on the health of a company's quality.

Quality audits are conducted in accordance with documented procedures and they provide assurance that the implementation and maintenance of the total quality system is in concert with the stipulated quality policies, objectives, plans and procedures.

Typically, a quality audit is a verification tool that identifies system weaknesses and potential problems and, in so doing, provides avenues for corrective action and system improvement. A quality system audit offers a wide range of benefits as it:

- Helps to develop an effective total quality system.
- Improves the overall management decision-making process.
- Assists in the optimal allocation of resources.
- Helps avoid potential problems.
- Allows timely corrective action.
- Reduces overhead and liability costs.
- Improves productivity and morale.
- Improves profitability, customer satisfaction and marketability.

◆ QUALITY AUDITS AND ISO-9000 CERTIFICATION

Quality auditing is an essential and integral part of ISO-9000 certification process. There are two types of quality audits involved in ISO-9000 certification:

- Internal quality audits
- External quality audits

Internal quality audits are performed on the company's own functions by the company's own personnel. They constitute an essential requirement for ISO-9000 certification. Companies seeking ISO-9000 certification have to develop their own strategic internal quality audit plans and procedures.

External quality audits are performed either on the suppliers to assess their capabilities in meeting specified requirements or on the customers to assess their needs and expectations. As indicated earlier, for a third-party certification to ISO-9000 quality system standards, the external quality audits are performed by the accredited registrars to assess the capabilities of the supplier to meet the requirements of the chosen level of standard.

Since auditing is a subject of profound importance to quality system management, the technical committee ISO/TC 176, is in the process of developing standards on auditing to supplement the ISO-9000 series. Thus far, the following standards have been developed:

- Guidelines for Auditing Quality Systems

  - Part 1: Auditing
  - Part 2: Qualification Criteria for Quality System Auditors
  - Part 3: Management of Audit Programs

This chapter, only briefly surveys the role of auditing within quality system management. For a detailed discussion on the subject, the reader is advised to consult the requisite standards or other useful sources and references.

◆ AUDITING FUNDAMENTALS

The definition of the term "Quality Audit" is given in the international standards, ISO-8402 and ISO-10011, is as follows:

> **"Quality Audit**: A systematic and independent examination to determine whether quality activities and related results comply with planned arrangements and whether these arrangements are implemented effectively and are suitable to achieve objectives."

Audits are normally carried out for one or more of the following purposes:

- To evaluate the effectiveness of the implemented quality system.
- To assess conformance to specified requirements.
- To identify shortcomings in the system.
- To identify improvement opportunities.

Quality system audits, whether internal or external, are performed with respect to a specific purpose and in accordance with a specified plan, procedure and criteria. There are different types of quality audits and, depending upon the need or the situation, one or several of them can be performed simultaneously. Following are the basic types to quality audits:

- System Audit: assessing how the quality management procedures are applied in practice and how effective they are.
- Product/Service Audit: evaluating the conformity of the product/service to specified technical requirements.
- Operational Audit: assessing the performance of a supplier/internal department or the needs/expectations of a customer.
- Process Audit: verifying how closely the established methods/procedures are followed in actual practice.
- Monitoring Audit: verifiying the processes to confirm that all parameters are maintained within their specifications.

◆ DEVELOPING INTERNAL AUDIT SYSTEM

One of the basic requirements for any company seeking ISO-9000 certification, is the establishment and implementation of a comprehensive quality audit system to verify conformance/effectiveness of the quality activities to the planned arrangements. Following are the basic steps in developing a quality audit system:

- Define the purpose and scope of the audit.
- Establish goals and objectives.
- Identify a management commitment and focus.
- Appoint a lead auditor given responsibility and authority to take action.
- Establish an audit team if required.
- Establish an overall planning framework for the audit system.
- Define the parameters and boundaries of each activity to be audited.
- Develop implementation plans.
- Develop and document audit plans, procedures and instructions.
- Identify resources and personnel.
- Establish priorities, action plans, and carry out the audits.
- Document the audit findings.
- Bring the audit results to the attention of the personnel having responsibility in the audited area.
- Take corrective/preventive action on the deficiencies identified by the audit.
- Assess the effectiveness of corrective action.
- Assess conformance to the specified requirements.
- Assess the effectiveness of the quality system.
- Identify opportunities and initiatives for improvement.

The success of an audit program is typically dependent on the following:

- A comprehensive audit plan: needs a total understanding of the quality system requirements and team effort.
- A detailed documented set of procedures and instructions: everyone must know, understand and follow uniform procedures.
- Qualified and objective auditors: requires extensive audit training.
- Thorough and unbiased reports: requires qualified personnel, commitment, training and independence of operability.
- Documentation and communication: requires an effective documentation system and reporting of deficiencies within and across all activities.
- Timely and effective corrective action: requires management commitment, resources, authority and total cooperation.
- System elements checklist: ensures that everything which required doing has been done; Chapter 9 provides a thorough and detailed checklist for this purpose.

◆ QUALITY AUDIT FRAMEWORK

A quality audit may be required in a variety of situations, such as a process audit, supplier audit, audit of the quality system within a company, audit by an external auditor vis-à-vis accreditation requirements or at the request of a company's management and/or a customer, etc. In each case, the fundamental requirement involves the establishment of a total audit procedural framework. Every audit procedure, whether for an internal audit or external audit, has a set of elements which must be addressed to develop the audit framework with an implementation plan. The following description of the quality audit system elements should provide sufficient assistance in developing an effective audit program. A flow chart of these system elements is schematically presented in Table 25.

Auditor

The effectiveness of the audit procedures and the confidence placed in them are highly dependent on the auditor's ability and expertise. The auditor must be well qualified, professionally proficient and adequately experienced in the subject. For the specific task at hand, the auditor's qualifications must be mutually acceptable to both the client requesting the audit and the auditing organization. Following are some of the general attributes that should be kept in mind in the selection of auditors:

- Competence in interpersonal and communication skills
- Ability to plan, organize, initiate, control and analyze
- Leadership abilities - to supervise, delegate, give direction and support
- Ability to work systematically, independently and judiciously
- Ability to use discretion regarding the confidentiality and proprietary of information and audit findings
- Balanced personality; absolute honesty and integrity; good attitude, conduct and appearance; self-confidence
- Ability to exercise independence of judgement

Auditee

It is the auditee's responsibility to ensure that the audit team has been provided with adequate working facilities, access to relevant information, and effective cooperation in all matters relating to the audit.

Audit Initiation

Before initiating the audit, the audit objectives must be set and agreed upon by the parties. Basically, the audit objectives should centre around verifying conformance to the stated policy, objectives/goals, system procedures and processes. The auditing organization must clearly identify the requisite audit resources commensurate with the task at hand, and plan all the other administrative details necessary to carry out the audit effectively.

Audit Planning

Typically, audit planning consists of the following activities:

- Review of auditee's provisions: quality system documentation, specifications, standards, etc.
- Audit timetable: audit dates, schedule of meetings, audit team composition and structure, activities to be audited and the requisite standard against which the audit is to be conducted
- Audit working papers: all relevant forms, records, checklists, assignment sheets, agenda items, etc. necessary for the conduct of the audit
- Compliance decision criteria: all the relevant criteria used in making a decision on the conformance/nonconformance of the quality system elements to the stipulated standard

Audit Implementation

Audit implementation involves the following components:

- An initial meeting between the auditor and auditeee management to clarify the overall plan for the conduct of the audit
- A detailed procedure for the conduct of the audit
- A mechanism for documenting and recording the audit findings
- A final meeting between the parties to discuss the nature and extent of noncompliance; how it shall be documented and reported; and a mutual agreement on the discontinuation of the audit.

Audit Report

The audit report is the document that formally communicates the findings of the audit to the client and the auditee. It must be prepared with great care and tenacity. It must be thorough and detailed and would normally identify the following items: the auditee, client and auditing organization, the audit dates, the audit standards, the audit team, the auditee's personnel contacted during the audit, the auditee's compliance status, the areas of noncompliance or of insufficient evidence, etc.

Corrective Action Follow-up

The objective here is to ensure that effective corrective action has been taken in every area of noncompliance. A follow-up procedure must be put in place to verify the effectiveness of the corrective action. Experience has indicated that companies who are able to develop self-correcting systems can effectively establish a constancy of compliance and improvement.

Record Retention

The objective here is to ensure that procedures have been clearly identified for the retention of audit records and documentation.

Confidentiality

Confidentiality is fundamental to all audit procedures. Consequently, a clear written agreement must be reached between the parties regarding the disclosure/nondisclosure of audit findings.

Table 25: Quality Audit System Elements

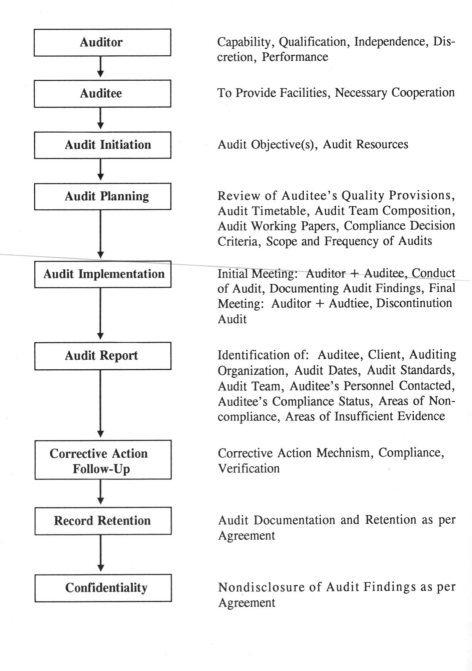

Auditor	Capability, Qualification, Independence, Discretion, Performance
Auditee	To Provide Facilities, Necessary Cooperation
Audit Initiation	Audit Objective(s), Audit Resources
Audit Planning	Review of Auditee's Quality Provisions, Audit Timetable, Audit Team Composition, Audit Working Papers, Compliance Decision Criteria, Scope and Frequency of Audits
Audit Implementation	Initial Meeting: Auditor + Auditee, Conduct of Audit, Documenting Audit Findings, Final Meeting: Auditor + Audtiee, Discontinution Audit
Audit Report	Identification of: Auditee, Client, Auditing Organization, Audit Dates, Audit Standards, Audit Team, Auditee's Personnel Contacted, Auditee's Compliance Status, Areas of Noncompliance, Areas of Insufficient Evidence
Corrective Action Follow-Up	Corrective Action Mechnism, Compliance, Verification
Record Retention	Audit Documentation and Retention as per Agreement
Confidentiality	Nondisclosure of Audit Findings as per Agreement

THIRTEEN

QUALITY SYSTEM GUIDELINES

♦ INTRODUCTION

A quality assurance manual for ISO-9000 certification needs to have at least the following characteristics:

- The manual has to address and accommodate, with precision, all the requirements stipulated in the chosen level of the ISO-9000 quality system standard.
- The manual has to describe, adequately and accurately, all the systems and procedures being physically functionally operated, followed and implemented in the company.
- The company should be in a position to produce documented objective evidence to validate the contents of the manual.

In order to develop and prepare a good manual, the manual writing team must have:

- A clear understanding of the requirements of the chosen ISO-9000 level of standard.
- A knowledge of all the systems and procedures operating in the company.
- The ability to write well and professionally.

Accurately deciphering and interpreting the requirements stipulated in any of the ISO-9000 series is almost imperative as preparation for ISO-9000 certification. Undoubtedly, the best way to achieve this is by studying the documents diligently over and over again. Preparing a checklist and guidelines on what is required to be addressed and how and in what sequence it will be accommodated, can facilitate the process.

Unfortunately, there are no guidelines and/or checklists yet available to assist the companies in this regard. The technical committee, ISO/TC 176, is in the process of developing such a set of guidelines (ISO/CD 9000-2: see the Bibliography), however, it would be some time before it is available for use. In this chapter, we are appending a set of guidelines that we have developed from our understanding, interpretation and experience and we hope this would help the many companies toiling to develop effective interpretation of the quality system requirements for ISO-9000 certification. We have chosen ISO-9001 as an example because this is the level with the highest set of requirements.

To be able to give an accurate and precise description of the system elements, the team members have to be well-informed about the systems and procedures operating in the company. Firstly, it is hoped that the make-up of the team is from those personnel who are well versed with the functioning of the organization. Notwithstanding however, no one person or group is expected to possess the complete understanding of all systems and procedures of the company. Therefore, in this regard the team would be continuously seeking assistance from other qualified personnel or functions of the organization either to obtain/validate information or to get the portions of the manual written. This also reinforces a need for conducting ISO-9000 awareness/training sessions for all employees so as to enable them to provide proper input and accurate information to the team and ultimately to the manual.

Finally, it is highly desirable that the team members would be thoroughly proficient and competent in the style of writing and command of language. The manual has to be written with utmost tenacity and professionalism. Besides being required for company use or ISO-9000 certification, the manual is an important marketing tool. To expedite the process and save time and resources, it may even be cost-effective for a company to consider hiring the services of a competent outside professional consultant. However, it must be clearly understood that a consultant can only act as a catalyst - the driving force must come from within the organization.

♦ QUALITY SYSTEM GUIDELINES

This section provides general guidelines and interpretation of the quality system requirements of ISO-9001. A clause-by-clause description and explanation of the requirements is appended, which should provide ample assistance in developing quality system documentation.

Before proceeding further, the following terminological interpretation used in the ISO-9001, ISO-9002 and ISO-9003 series of contractual/external standards, should be noted:

- "Supplier" refers to your company or organization.
- "Purchaser" refers to your customers, ie., companies to whom you provide products and services.
- "Sub-contractor" refers to companies supplying raw materials, products and services to you.

Unfortunately, however, the same terminology is not followed in ISO-9004: Quality Management Guidelines (Internal). The usage of terms in this document is as follows:

- "Company" refers to your company or organization.
- "Customer" refers to companies to whom you provide products/services.
- "Supplier" refers to companies supplying products/services to you.

Clause 4.1: Management Responsibility

This is the start of systems elements in ISO-9001. This clause is quite long and it sets the overall scene. First, it requires senior management to define and establish its quality policy and objectives and to commit itself to them. The policy and objectives must be effectively communicated throughout the organization. They must be clearly understood, implemented and maintained at all levels in the organization. The driving force behind all this, however, is the chief executive officer. He has the ultimate authority and responsibility for quality in the organization.

For managing the quality system effectively, the clause requires a clear definition and delineation of responsibility, authority and interrelationship of all personnel affecting the quality of products and services to customers. The emphasis is on preventing nonconforming products from occurring, controlling when it happens, identifying and recording quality problems and issues, recommending solutions, taking corrective action and verifying the implementation and effectiveness of actions taken.

Next, the clause requires the identification of appropriate resources and trained personnel to carry out the verification task. Verification includes monitoring and auditing the quality system and all other associated activities such as: checking out product design, testing and inspecting during processing, checking of installation, repair or servicing work, etc. The clause also insists that verification should be carried out by personnel independent of those who have direct responsibility for the work being done.

Clause 4.1 also requires the appointment of a management representative charged with the authority and responsibility to ensure effective implementation and maintenance of the system.

Finally, the clause requires regular management reviews of the system to ensure its continuing suitability and effectiveness. The management representative and/or the manager of quality program, in conjunction with the internal auditor, would initiate, arrange and accomplish reviews of the quality system through the Steering Committee and Process Improvement Team meetings. Records of these reviews must be maintained to facilitate and authorize improve-ments in the system.

Clause 4.2: Quality System

This is a general clause that emphasizes the need for the system to be properly documented via the various levels of documentation, viz., Quality Manual, Procedures Manuals, Work Instructions, and all the requisite forms, records, books proformas, etc. A quality plan must be established to identify the requirements of the system, the methods and equipment, the personnel and resources, the controls to be exercised, and the records and documentation required to prove the effective implementation, operation and maintenance of the system.

Clause 4.3: Contract Review

This clause is meant to ensure that the company clearly understands the customer's needs and expectations and has the requisite resources to meet those requirements. Whether the requirements are simple or complex, they must be clearly defined, documented and agreed upon between the customer and the supplier.

Clause 4.4: Design Control

This clause is applicable only to ISO-9001 and pertains to products and services which involve significant in-house technical design and development content. To satisfy the clause, the organization must establish design and development plan to identify design input/output requirements, assign appropriate personnel and resources for each design activity, and ensure complete interface between various functions and activities, including input and feedback from the customer. Design control procedures must be established to include methods for design review, changes, verification and documentation of all design and development activities.

Clause 4.5: Document Control

This is a general clause requiring the documentation of all systems elements and activities. The clause requires that all documents be adequate and correct for their purpose and available at all appropriate work locations. All documents must be properly approved before they are issued. The same applies to revisions, changes and modifications made to documents. It is also important to ensure that obsolete issues are promptly removed from use and replaced by revised and approved ones. A master list must be kept of the latest editions in circulation and the changes or revisions.

Clause 4.6: Purchasing

This clause is very important because to produce right in the first place depends on receiving the right quality material. The company must do all it can to ensure that the purchased raw materials conform to specified requirements. The clause emphasizes focusing attention on three main elements in purchasing: assessment and selection of sub-contractors, accuracy of purchasing document, and the verification of purchased products.

To receive the right material, it is imperative to ensure that the purchase order describes complete and accurate information about the product ordered. The company must thoroughly review and approve the ordering documents for adequacy of specified requirements before they are sent to the sub-contractor. The company should select sub-contractors on the basis of their ability to meet the quality levels expected of them and keep a record of their capabilities and performance. The company should have the right to check the suitability of supplies bought either at source or upon receipt. Also, acceptance of the purchased product does not absolve the sub-contractor of the responsibility to continuously provide acceptable product.

Clause 4.7: Purchaser Supplied Product

This clause relates to the situation where the customer actually provides items or materials for incorporation in the goods he ultimately buys back. The supplier has the responsibility to make sure that the purchaser supplied products are suitable for the purpose and are in good condition. If they are not, this has to be identified and reported back to the customer.

Clause 4.8: Product Identification and Traceability

This clause emphasizes the need to establish procedures for tracing specific materials or assemblies throughout the process of their development, from procurement to production, delivery and/or installation. Traceability may be necessary for reasons of safety or regulatory requirements. An obvious method for identification and traceability would be a serial numbering system relating back to an inspection status record.

Clause 4.9: Process Control

Process control is at the heart of Total Quality Management. Quality cannot be inspected into a product; it has to be embedded and infused into a product by a continuous process control and improvement effort. This clause, therefore, requires the organization to identify the processing steps needed to produce the product and to set out a plan for implementing them.

The clause recommends that processes should be carried out under controlled conditions which include: use of documented work instructions, reference standards/codes and quality plans; control of process/product characteristics; suitable equipment and work conditions, etc. The clause also requires that particular care be exercised for those special processes where the product characteristics are difficult to measure or verify in subsequent inspections, but where processing deficiencies may become apparent only after the product is in use. Special attention should be given for continuous monitoring of such processes to ensure conformance to specified requirements and prevention of deficiencies.

Clause 4.10: Inspection and Testing

Inspection and testing is an integral part of most production situations and relates to receiving of goods, in-process production and final inspection.

Purchased material must be inspected in accordance with the quality plan or documented procedures to ensure conformance to specified requirements before it is released for processing. The nature and extent of receiving inspection would, indeed, depend on the nature of controls exercised at source and/or on documented evidence of quality conformance provided. In cases where there is an urgency of release of raw material for production, the company should make a positive identification and keep records of the material so as to recall or replace it in the event of nonconformance.

The clause also requires that inspection, tests, process monitoring and control methods must be used during the processing phase to establish product conformance/nonconformance. The principles of final inspection and testing are the same. The product should go through a final inspection and testing routine in whatever detail may be necessary to make sure it meets the specification required by the customer. It should not be delivered until this has been done. The clause emphasizes the establishment and maintenance of records to provide evidence that the product has passed inspection and/or test with defined acceptance criteria.

Clause 4.11: Inspection, Measuring and Test Equipment

The efficacy of inspection and test results can hardly be relied upon unless the equipment being used is suitable and accurate. This clause, therefore, addresses the need for ensuring that the inspection, measuring and test equipment is capable of the accuracy and precision necessary.

All inspection, measuring and test equipment and devices that can affect product quality has to be checked at prescribed intervals and recalibrated if it is out of adjustment. The calibration should be in accordance with a nationally recognized standard or a clearly documented method where no such standard exists. Records of the checks and any recalibration and adjustment must be kept. This clause goes on further to make other simple, sensible stipulations relating to calibration, such as: suitability of environmental conditions, proper handling and storage facilities, safeguards against tampering, etc.

Clause 4.12: Inspection and Test Status

This clause requires that a recognizable indicator be affixed to the product to identify the inspection and testing routines it has gone through and its status of conformance/nonconformance to the specified requirements. The indicator may be a mark on the product, a tag or a sticker attached to it, and it may also show who authorized its quality status and its release for delivery.

Clause 4.13: Control of Nonconforming Product

This clause requires the establishment and maintenance of procedures and controls to ensure that nonconforming products are prevented from inadvertent use or installation. Essentially, products identified to be nonconforming should be segregated and reported to the appropriate function.

Nonconforming product may be reworked to meet the specification, regraded, or it may be scrapped. The proposed use or repair of nonconforming product should be reported for concession to the customer and the nature of nonconformity recorded. Repaired and reworked product should be re-inspected as per documented procedures.

Clause 4.14: Corrective Action

Essential to the effective implementation of quality system and continuous quality improvement is the understanding of what must be done when things go wrong and how to prevent them from reoccuring. This clause requires the organization to investigate and analyze the cause of nonconforming products and take action to prevent it from happening again. Records of investigation must be kept and controls instituted to ensure that corrective actions are taken and that they are effective.

The clause, in fact, goes further to recommend a more proactive role by means of analysis of quality records, service reports, customer complaints, and similar information as a basis for anticipating potential nonconforming products and preventing it from reoccurring.

Clause 4.15: Handling, Storage, Packaging and Delivery

This clause simply demands that the organization should establish effective procedures for handling, storing, packing and delivery of products. These procedures should be designed to prevent damage or deterioration to the product.

Clause 4.16: Quality Records

The scope of this clause spans over the entire quality system, and reconfirms the importance of documentation as a vital factor in demonstrating that the system is being operated as per quality policy, objectives and plans. Quality records must be maintained throughout the cycle of production, from records relating to purchased material and sub-contracted work to design, production, process control, inspection, delivery and installation. Records must be legible and clearly referenced with the product or service they relate to. They must also be stored effectively and protected from loss or damage. Retention times of quality records must be established, sometimes in consultation with the customer, and recorded. In some cases, the contract allows the customer access to the quality records.

Clause 4.17: Internal Quality Audits

Auditing is fundamental to quality assessment. A quality audit is an objective evaluation of the effectiveness of the quality system. The clause requires that a company conducts a comprehensive system of planned and documented internal quality audits to verify system effectiveness and to ensure that the implementation and maintenance of the quality system is in concert with the stipulated quality policies, objectives, plans and procedures. Each aspect of the system is audited according to its importance to the overall quality objective.

The Manager of Quality Program and/or the Management Representative is responsible for arranging and coordinating the audits. The audit findings are documented and brought to the attention of the personnel having responsibility in the area audited as well as reported to the management. Timely corrective action is appropriately taken on the deficiencies found by the audit.

Clause 4.18: Training

The standard makes 'training' an integral part of the Total Quality Management (TQM) system. The quality of products and services is highly dependent on the ability of personnel to perform their tasks. The clause requires the organization to identify training and education needs and set-up training programs to maintain, update and enhance the knowledge and skills of the personnel. Like any other aspect of the system, appropriate records of training should be maintained for audit and review.

Clause 4.19: Servicing

This clause is obvious and is intended to make it clear that if the organization provides servicing for its customers, in the sense of equipment maintenance, for example, then it should establish effective procedures for carrying it out and monitoring its quality to those required in production and installation.

Clause 4.20: Statistical Techniques

Statistical methods provide the most fundamental tools for process control and improvement and for verifying the acceptability of process capability and product characteristics. Although this clause is relatively short, it still lays sufficient emphasis on establishing procedures to identify and use appropriate statistical techniques to analyze data and information in all activity areas that affect quality. Statistical techniques may include such methods as: sampling inspection plans, control chart methods, design of experiments, etc.

◆ QUALITY MANUAL GUIDELINES

The most crucial tasks for ISO-9000 Certification is the preparation of the quality manual. However, before this mammoth task can be undertaken, it is imperative to have an absolutely thorough understanding of the requirements of the standard. The previous section was meant to provide a good general understanding of the requirements, with ISO-9001 as an example. In this section, we are now providing a detailed package of guidelines describing the requirements stipulated in each clause of ISO-9001. We have specifically chosen a sequential step-by-step format of presentation of the guidelines so as to facilitate clause-by-clause writing of the manual. Note that in some cases, our interpretation simply amounts to rewording of the ISO-9001 clause element - it is because the clause interpretation is simple but has been included as a reminder to ensure that the manual would adequately cover the requisite element.

For each clause of ISO-9001, the guidelines identify what must be addressed and included in the quality manual. The personnel or team writing the manual should, therefore, take each item one by one and identify the corresponding systems and procedures that are or should be operating in the company. Continuing in this manner, it should not be difficult to complete the Quality Manual that adequately and accurately describes the company's quality system while effectively addressing all the requirements stipulated in ISO-9001.

The guidelines for the clause-by-clause interpretation of the systems elements have been particularly presented in a bullet format to facilitate the writing of the manual. The bullets identify the requirements of the clause and as such the manual should follow the sequence of short, precise and accurate paragraphs addressing each requirement. For each clause, therefore, the manual should adequately address all the requirements of the clause while describing the requisite system element physically and functionally operating in the company. Long descriptions of the system or procedures or any motherhood statements about them should be avoided as far as practical.

ISO-9001: QUALITY SYSTEM REQUIREMENTS

SYSTEM ELEMENTS (*Clause*)
Manual Guidelines

4.1 MANAGEMENT RESPONSIBILITY

- Define quality policy and objectives.
- Establish quality organizational structure.
- Provide verification resources.
- Appoint a management representative.
- Plan for management review of the quality system.

4.1.1 Quality Policy

The supplier's management shall define and document its policy and objectives for, and commitment to, quality. The supplier shall ensure that this policy is understood, implemented and maintained at all levels in the organization.

- Define and document policy and objectives.
- Policy to include: elements of management commitment; approach to product/service quality.
- Policy means: total customer satisfaction; product/service quality constancy and conformance to specified requirements.
- Policy to be: understood by everyone; implemented and maintained at all levels within the organization.
- Objectives to be: measurable; ambitious; achievable.
- Commitment can be demonstrated by: ensuring that everyone understands and implements the quality policy; initiating, managing and following-up on the implementation of quality policy and system; not accepting deviations from policy, poor quality or wasted resources.
- Policy and objectives should be such as to address all requisite ISO-9001 system elements.

4.1.2   Organization

4.1.2.1   Responsibility and Authority

The responsibility, authority and the interrelation of all personnel who manage, perform and verify work affecting quality shall be defined; particularly for personnel who need the organizational freedom and authority to

a)   initiate action to prevent the occurrence of product nonconformity;
b)   identify and record any product quality problems;
c)   initiate, recommend or provide solutions through designated channels;
d)   verify the implementation of solutions;
e)   control further processing, delivery or installation of nonconforming product until the deficiency or unsatisfactory condition has been corrected.

- Define and document responsibility and authority of people who manage, perform and verify the work.
- Prepare the organizational chart identifying their inter-relationship.
- Ensure that the responsibility and authority is in line with company policy and objectives, and all relevant personnel are fully aware of the channels of responsibility.
- Ensure that the designated personnel have the freedom and authority to: identify and record quality problems; initiate, recommend and provide solutions through the system; verify the implementation of solutions; institute further control mechanisms to prevent nonconformance.
- Responsible persons must constantly interface with all activities and links which influence the achievement of quality, such as: purchasing, design development, production, process control, inspection, marketing, sales, delivery, servicing.
- Quality is everyone's responsibility through: effective and timely work habits; checking and inspection of all requisite documentation, procedures, specifications, tools and material; identification of output deficiencies and taking of prompt corrective and preventive action.
- The ultimate responsibility for quality rests with the management: to display commitment; to promote awareness; to organize work; to provide resources; to ensure customer satisfaction.

4.1.2.2 Verification Resources and Personnel

The supplier shall identify in-house verification requirements, provide adequate resources and assign trained personnel for verification activities (see 4.18).

Verification activities shall include inspection, test and monitoring of the design, production, installation and servicing processes and/or product; design reviews and audits of the quality system, processes and/or product shall be carried out by personnel independent of those having direct responsibility for the work being performed.

- Identify in-house verification requirements.
- Provide trained personnel and adequate resources.
- Verification activities include: inspection, test and monitoring of the design, production, installation and servicing processes and/or product; design reviews and audit of the quality system processes and/or product.
- Verification activities (process, product or system audit) should be carried out by staff independent of those having direct responsibility for the work being performed.
- Verification resources also involve: proper information regarding verification activities and arrangements; awareness of existing standards; training for the people involved; necessary equipment; sufficient time to do the work; documented procedures; cooperation of everyone involved in verification work.

4.1.2.3 Management Representative

The supplier shall appoint a management representative who, irrespective of other responsibilities, shall have defined authority and responsibility for ensuring that the requirements of this International Standard are implemented and maintained.

- Management to appoint a quality representative with the authority and responsibility to ensure that: the quality system is developed, implemented and maintained in all functions; quality strategy and improvement programs are prepared and followed up; inspection/audit of products, processes and quality system is carried out effectively.
- The representative is not responsible for the quality of the product per sè, but ensures effective implementation of quality improvement systems and processes.
- The appointment of the management representative is recorded in the Quality Manual and all relevant personnel are made aware of this appointment and its associated authority and responsibility.

4.1.3 Management Review

The quality system adopted to satisfy the requirements of this International Standard shall be reviewed at appropriate intervals by the supplier's management to ensure its continuing suitability and effectiveness. Records of such reviews shall be maintained (see 4.16).

NOTE – Management reviews normally include assessment of the results of internal quality audits, but are carried out by, or on behalf of, the supplier's management; viz management personnel having direct responsibility for the system. (See 4.17).

- Identify the company's quality review process in the manual.
- Management should review the quality system at regular intervals to ensure its continuing suitability and effectiveness.
- Results of these reviews should be: documented, analyzed for deficiencies and problems; discussed with responsible personnel.
- Suitable and appropriate corrective/preventive action should be taken to eliminate system deficiencies.
- Management reviews should include details of: adequacy of organizational structure and resources for the effective implementation of quality system; the extent and degree of implementation of the quality system; the performance status of processes and systems; the actual product/service quality status; and other strategic information based on: internal audits, costs, customer feedback, quality costs, rate and frequency of nonconformances, effectiveness of corrective action, training needs, etc.

4.2 QUALITY SYSTEM

The supplier shall establish and maintain a documented quality system as a means of ensuring that product conforms to specified requirements. This shall include

a)   the preparation of documented quality system procedures and instructions in accordance with the requirements of this International Standard;
b)   the effective implementation of the documented quality system procedures and instructions.

NOTE - In meeting specified requirements, timely consideration needs to be given to the following activities:

a)   the preparation of quality plans and a quality manual in accordance with the specified requirements;
b)   the identification and acquisition of any controls, processes, inspection equipment, fixtures, total production resources and skills that may be needed to achieve the required quality;
c)   the updating, as necessary, of quality control, inspection and testing techniques, including the development of new instrumentation;
d)   the identification of any measurement requirement involving capability that exceeds the known state of the art in sufficient time for the needed capability to be developed;
e)   the clarification of standards of acceptability for all features and requirements, including those which contain a subjective element;
f)   the compatibility of the design, the production process, installation, inspection and test procedures and the applicable documentation;
g)   the identification and preparation of quality records (see 4.16).

- This clause is meant to provide guidelines for establishing a quality system to meet ISO-9001 requirements.

- A quality system needs to be established, maintained and documented. The system covers the organization, allocation of responsibilities, procedures, processes and resources which would jointly lead to the provision of goods and services in accordance with the quality policy and objectives.
- The quality system normally is documented by means of one or several tiers of documents, eg., a Quality Manual as an overall system manual; one or more specific procedural manuals for each component of the production process; requisite work instructions; and suitable forms, books, files and records.
- The Quality Manual defines and identifies the scope of quality plans, quality system procedures and review mechanism as per requirements of ISO-9001.
- Make sure that the manual properly addresses all the requisite elements appended in the "Note" to clause 4.2.

4.3 CONTRACT REVIEW

The supplier shall establish and maintain procedures for contract review and for the coordination of these activities. Each contract shall be reviewed by the supplier to ensure that

a)   the requirements are adequately defined and documented;
b)   any requirements differing from those in the tender are resolved;
c)   the supplier has the capability to meet contractual requirements.

Records of such contract reviews shall be maintained (see 4.16).

Note - The contract review activities, interfaces and communication within the supplier's organization should be coordinated with the purchaser's organization, as appropriate.

- Review the contract to ensure that: the purchase order requirements are clear, adequately defined and properly documented; any discrepancy between the requirements and tender is resolved; the supplier has the capability and capacity to meet the contractual requirements.

- Contract review records must be maintained.
- Results of the review should be discussed with the purchaser in order to achieve agreement.
- All requisite findings of the review should be communicated to the departments that needs it.
- A review process plan/checklist should be developed to standardize and improve the contract review process.

4.4 DESIGN CONTROL

4.4.1 General

The supplier shall establish and maintain procedures to control and verify the design of the product in order to ensure that the specified requirements are met.

- Identify, clause by clause, all the requisite design control procedures operating in the company.
- Design function may comprise various facets: product design, process design, service design.
- Develop and maintain control and verification procedures for all phases of the design function process.

4.4.2 Design and Development Planning

The supplier shall draw up plans that identify the responsibility for each design and development activity. The plans shall describe or reference these activities and shall be updated as the design evolves.

- Establish and document a plan for all activities relating to design and development work.
- The plan should identify work schedules, verification activities, as well as assignment of the relevant responsibilities.
- Integrate the plan with other relevant plans and verification procedures.
- The plans must be updated as the design evolves.

4.4.2.1   Activity Assignment

The design and verification activities shall be planned and assigned to qualified personnel equipped with adequate resources.

- Assign qualified personnel, with responsibilities for specific work functions, to the planned design and verification activities.
- Provide adequate resources.

4.4.2.2   Organizational and Technical Interfaces

Organizational and technical interfaces between different groups shall be identified and the necessary information documented, transmitted and regularly reviewed.

- Establish inter and intra-organizational and technical interface between various design work groups associated with the process as well as product.
- Ensure that the necessary design information is documented, transmitted and reviewed on a regular basis.

4.4.3   Design Input

Design input requirements relating to the product shall be identified, documented and their selection reviewed by the supplier for adequacy.

Incomplete, ambiguous or conflicting requirements shall be resolved with those responsible for drawing up these requirements.

- The manual should indicate all design input procedures.
- Identify, review and record all pertinent design inputs related to the product in a design description document.
- Design description should be all encompassing, to include design aspects, materials and processes requiring development and analysis, including any prototype testing, verification, installation and service.
- Incomplete, ambiguous or conflicting requirements must be resolved and agreements reached between purchaser and supplier on how the design requirements will be met.

- Establish a schedule for verification, review and update of design requirements.

4.4.4 Design Output

Design output shall be documented and expressed in terms of requirements, calculations and analyses.

Design output shall

a) meet the design input requirements;
b) contain or reference acceptance criteria;
c) conform to appropriate regulatory requirements whether or not these have been stated in the input information;
d) identify those characteristics of the design that are crucial to the safe and proper functioning of the product.

- Identify and document design output in terms of requirements, calculations and analyses, such as drawings, specifications, instructions, software, installation, service procedures, and bills of materials.
- Design outputs should exhibit how they embody design input requirements, including a reference acceptance criteria.
- Design outputs must conform to all regulatory requirements.
- Design outputs must identify those characteristics that are crucial to the safe functioning of the product.

4.4.5 Design Verification

The supplier shall plan, establish, document and assign to competent personnel functions for verifying the design.

Design verification shall establish that design output meets the design input requirement (see 4.4.4) by means of design control measures such as:

a) holding and recording design reviews (see 4.16);
b) undertaking qualification tests and demonstrations;

c) *carrying out alternative calculations;*
d) *comparing the new design with a similar proven design, if available.*

- Plan, establish and document design review and verification activities.
- Assign qualified personnel.
- Verification is done to check that the design: satisfies all specified product/service requirements; meets functional and operational requirements (eg., performance, reliability, maintainability); covers safety and other environmental considerations; ensures compatibility and interfaces of materials, components, and/or service elements; has considered selection of appropriate materials and facilities; has ensured technical feasibility of plans for implementing the design portions of the contract (eg., procurement, production, inspection, testing); will allow consistent achievement of tolerances.
- Ensure that proper design verification methods are employed, such as: holding and recording design reviews; undertaking qualification tests and demonstrations; carrying out alternative calculations; comparison of new designs with similar proven designs (if available).

4.4.6 Design Changes

The supplier shall establish and maintain procedures for the identification, documentation and appropriate review and approval of all changes and modifications.

- Establish procedures to ensure that all changes and modifications have been identified, documented, reviewed, approved, and effectively disseminated.
- Design changes/modifications can arise due to: omissions, errors, material selection, manufacturing difficulties, improvement requirements, safety considerations, purchaser requested changes.

4.5 DOCUMENT CONTROL

4.5.1 Document Approval and Issue

The supplier shall establish and maintain procedures to control all documents and data that relate to the requirements of this International Standard. These documents shall be reviewed and approved for adequacy by authorized personnel prior to issue. This control shall ensure that

a)   *the pertinent issues of appropriate documents are available at all locations where operations essential to the effective functioning of the quality system are performed;*
b)   *obsolete documents are promptly removed from all points of issue or use.*

- List all document control procedures in the manual.
- Establish and maintain procedures to control all documentation and data pertaining to the quality system.
- Ensure that the following documents are reviewed and approved for adequacy prior to issue:
  - Quality Manual and System Procedures
  - Quality Plans
  - Documents pertaining to: Design, Purchasing, Process Control, Audit.
- Ensure the availability of pertinent issues of all appropriate documents at all essential locations.
- Obsolete documents should be promptly removed from all points of issue or use.

4.5.2   Document Changes/Modifications

Changes to documents shall be reviewed and approved by the same functions/ organizations that performed the original review and approval unless specifically designated otherwise. The designated organizations shall have access to pertinent background information upon which to base their review and approval.

Where practicable, the nature of the change shall be identified in the document or the appropriate attachments.

A master list or equivalent document control procedure shall be established to identify the current revision of documents in order to preclude the use of non-applicable documents.

Documents shall be re-issued after a practical number of changes have been made.

- Establish and maintain a continuous and viable mechanism for controlling document changes/revisions.
- Changes must be reviewed/approved by the same functions/ organizations who performed the original review/approval (unless specifically designated otherwise). Pertinent background information must be available on which to base changes/reviews/ approvals.
- Assessment of the effect of changes on other related procedures, systems, product/service must be made and appropriate action taken. The nature of these changes must be identified in the document or appropriate attachments.
- Notice of changes must be sent, and confirmation received through transmittal record form, to all persons who have been issued a copy of the Quality Manual.
- Develop a document control procedure to identify current revision of documents, and to preclude the use of non-applicable documents.
- Revise documents after a practical number of changes have been made.

4.6 PURCHASING

4.6.1 General

The supplier shall ensure that purchased product conforms to specified requirements.

- List, in the manual, all requisite procurement procedures of the company.
- Plan and establish a system/procedure to control all procurement activity to ensure that purchased products meets specified requirements.

4.6.2 Assessment of Subcontractors

The supplier shall select sub-contractors on the basis of their ability to meet sub-contract requirements, including quality requirements. The supplier shall establish and maintain records of acceptable sub-contractors (see 4.16).

The selection of sub-contractors, and the type and extent of control exercised by the supplier, shall be dependent upon the type of product and, where appropriate, on records of sub-contractors' previously demonstrated capability and performance.

The supplier shall ensure that quality system controls are effective.

- Establish and maintain a system for choosing satisfactory sub-contractors, based on:
  - Review of past performance in supplying similar products/services.
  - Ability to meet sub-contract requirements, including quality capability.
  - Maintenance of an appropriate quality system for processes/products/services.
- Sub-contractors' performance must be reviewed at regular intervals, commensurate with the complexity and technical requirements of the product.
- Establish and maintain records of acceptable sub-contractors.

4.6.3 Purchasing Data

Purchasing documents shall contain data clearly describing the product ordered, including, where applicable,

a) the type, class, style, grade or other precise identification;

b) the title or other positive identi-fication, and applicable issue of specifications, drawings, process requirements, inspection instructions and other relevant technical data, including requirements for approval or qualification of product, procedures, process equipment and personnel;

c) the title, number and issue of the quality system International Standard to be applied to the product.

The supplier shall review and approve purchasing documents for adequacy of specified requirements prior to release.

- Establish and maintain an effective procurement data system.
- Purchasing documents should clearly describe all the technical requirements (type, class or other precise information) to ensure the quality of the procured products/services.
- The purchase order should reference to the quality standard applied and identify all technical requirements, including testing/process requirements.
- Review and approve purchasing documents for adequacy of specified requirements prior to release.

4.6.4   Verification of Purchased Product

Where specified in the contract, the purchaser or his representative shall be afforded the right to verify at source or upon receipt that purchased product conforms to specified requirements. Verification by the purchaser shall not absolve the supplier of the responsibility to provide acceptable product nor shall it preclude subsequent rejection.

When the purchaser or his representative elects to carry out verification at the sub-contractor's plant, such verification shall not be used by the supplier as evidence of effective control of quality by the sub-contractor.

- The manual should identify procedures for verification of purchased product.
- Procedures and requirements for product verification must be specified in the contract.
- The purchaser must have the right to verify the product at source or upon receipt. The details of verification process, ie., intensity and frequency of inspection, location of inspection, etc., can be established in concurrence with the sub-contractor.
- Records of verification activities should be maintained, including of corrective action taken, if any.
- Verification by the purchaser does not absolve the sub-contractor of the responsibility to continuously provide acceptable product.

- Notwithstanding the verification process, the sub-contractor must continuously use effective process control methods to improve the quality of products supplied.

4.7 PURCHASER SUPPLIED PRODUCT

The supplier shall establish and maintain procedures for verification, storage and maintenance of purchaser supplied product provided for incorporation into supplies. Any such product that is lost, damaged or is otherwise unsuitable for use shall be recorded and reported to the purchaser (see 4.16).

NOTE - Verification by the supplier does not absolve the purchaser of the respon-sibility to provide acceptable product.

- "Purchaser supplied products" are products owned by the customer and furnished to the supplier for inclusion into the final product to meet the requirements of the contract. It may be a product or service, for example, the use of a customer's transport for delivery, use of machine tools or equipment, etc.
- The purchaser bears the responsibility of providing acceptable product or service.
- The supplier should establish and maintain procedures for product/ service verification, storage, and maintenance of these "purchaser supplied products".
- The supplier must report to the purchaser, any loss, damage or unsuitability of the supplied product/service.

4.8 PRODUCT IDENTIFICATION AND TRACEABILITY

Where appropriate, the supplier shall establish and maintain procedures for identifying the product from applicable drawings, specifications or other documents, during all stages of production, delivery and installation.

Where, and to the extent that, trace-ability is a specified requirement,

individual product or batches shall have
a unique identification. This identi-
fication shall be recorded (see 4.16).

- Establish, maintain and document the process of identification and traceability of the product during all stages of procurement, production, delivery and installation.
- Identification is made to the applicable drawings, specifications or part number.
- Establish individual batch or lot identification when specifically required.
- Record the identification needed for traceability at all pertinent stages.

4.9 PROCESS CONTROL

4.9.1 General

The supplier shall identify and plan the
production and, where applicable, instal-
lation processes which directly affect
quality and shall ensure that these
processes are carried out under controlled
conditions. Controlled conditions shall
include the following:

a) documented work instructions defining
the manner of production and instal-
lation, where the absence of such
instructions would adversely affect
quality, use of suitable production
and installation equipment, suitable
working environment, compliance with
reference standards/codes and quality
plans;

b) monitoring and control of suitable
process and product characteristics
during production and installation;

c) the approval of processes and equipment,
as appropriate;

d) criteria for workmanship which shall be
stipulated, to the greatest practicable
extent, in written standards or by means
of representative samples.

- Identify all process control activities pursued in the company.

- Quality has to be manufactured in, and this is accomplished through effective process control systems.
- Plan and operate production and installation processes (where applicable) under controlled conditions.
- Implementing controlled conditions imply:
  - Documented work instructions, process flow charts, standardized criteria for workmanship.
  - Use of statistical process control (SPC) techniques.
  - Approval of processes before and during use.
  - Monitoring and control of product and process characteristics during production in order to prevent nonconformities.

4.9.2 Special Processes

These are processes, the results of which cannot be fully verified by subsequent inspection and testing of the product and where, for example, processing deficiencies may become apparent only after the product is in use. Accordingly, continuous monitoring and/or compliance with documented procedures is required to ensure that the specified requirements are met. These processes shall be qualified and shall also comply with the requirements of 4.9.1.

Records shall be maintained for qualified processes, equipment and personnel, as appropriate.

- Special processes are those that the results of which cannot be verified by subsequent inspection or test, but deficiencies may become apparent during use.
- Identify special processes in the Quality Manual.
- Plan, implement and monitor controlled conditions for special processes the same way as done for other processes in accordance with 4.9.1 above.
- Maintain records of qualified processes, personnel and equipment.

4.10 INSPECTION AND TESTING

4.10.1 Receiving Inspection and Testing

4.10.1.1 *The supplier shall ensure that incoming product is not used or processed (except in the circumstances described in 4.10.1.2) until it has been inspected or otherwise verified as conforming to specified requirements. Verification shall be in accordance with the quality plan or documented procedures.*

4.10.1.2 *Where incoming product is released for urgent production purposes, it shall be positively identified and recorded (see 4.16) in order to permit immediate recall and replacement in the event of nonconformance to specified requirements.*

NOTE - In determining the amount and nature of receiving inspection, consideration should be given to the control exercised at source and documented evidence of quality conformance provided.

- Establish a quality plan or documented procedures (sampling inspection plans, etc.) to verify incoming product before it is used for processing.
- Establish procedures to handle nonconforming product as per clause 4.13 of ISO-9001 pertaining to control of nonconforming product.
- Product may be released, without incoming inspection, under positive recall. Product to be identified and recorded for traceability or inspection at a later date as per quality plan.
- The intensity and frequency of receiving inspection can be minimized by ensuring and exercising controls at the source.

4.10.2 In-process Inspection and Testing

The supplier shall

a) inspect, test and identify product as required by the quality plan or documented procedures;

b) *establish product conformance to specified requirements by use of process monitoring and control methods;*

c) *hold product until the required inspection and tests have been completed or necessary reports have been received and verified except when product is released under positive recall procedures (see 4.10.1). Release under positive recall procedures shall not preclude the activities outlined in 4.10.2a;*

d) *identify nonconforming product.*

- Establish and identify in the manual, the quality plan or documented procedures for in-process inspection and testing.
- Use process control methods to monitor process quality and conformance to specified requirements.
- Hold product or use positive recall.
- Handle nonconformities as per procedures established in the Quality Manual.

4.10.3   Final Inspection and Testing

The quality plan or documented procedures for final inspection and testing shall require that all specified inspection and tests, including those specified either on receipt of product or in-process, have been carried out and that the data meets specified requirements.

The supplier shall carry out all final inspection and testing in accordance with the quality plan or documented procedures to complete the evidence of conformance of the finished product to the specified requirements.

No product shall be despatched until all the activities specified in the quality plan or documented procedures have been satisfactorily completed and the associated data and documentation is available and authorized.

- Establish and identify, in the manual, all procedures for final inspection and testing.
- The quality plan or documented procedures should require that all of the following inspections have been carried out:
  - Incoming inspection
  - In-process inspection
  - Final inspection
- The inspection results and data must indicate product conformance to specified requirements.
- Product should not be shipped until the inspection results are complete and specified requirements are met.
- Handle nonconformities as per procedures established in the Quality Manual.

4.10.4   Inspection and Test Records

The supplier shall establish and maintain records which give evidence that the product has passed inspection and/or test with defined acceptance criteria (see 4.16).

- Maintain records to verify that the product has passed inspection and meets acceptance criteria.
- This clause also interfaces with clause 4.16, which requires that all quality records must be maintained.

4.11   INSPECTION, MEASURING AND TEST EQUIPMENT

The supplier shall control, calibrate and maintain inspection, measuring and test equipment, whether owned by the supplier, on loan, or provided by the purchaser, to demonstrate the conformance of product to the specified requirements. Equipment shall be used in a manner which ensures that measurement uncertainty is known and is consistent with the required measurement capability.

The supplier shall

a) identify the measurements to be made, the accuracy required and select the appropriate inspection, measuring and test equipment;

b) identify, calibrate and adjust all inspection, measuring and test equipment and devices that can affect product quality at prescribed intervals, or prior to use, against certified equipment having a known valid relationship to nationally recognized standards - where no such standards exist, the basis used for calibration shall be documented;

c) establish, document and maintain calibration procedures, including details of equipment type, identification number, location, frequency of checks, check method, acceptance criteria and the action to be taken when results are unsatisfactory;

d) ensure that the inspection, measuring and test equipment is capable of the accuracy and precision necessary;

e) identify inspection, measuring and test equipment with a suitable indicator or approved identification record to show the calibration status;

f) maintain calibration records for inspection, measuring and test equipment (see 4.16);

g) assess and document the validity of previous inspection and test results when inspection, measuring and test equipment is found to be out of calibration;

h) ensure that the environmental conditions are suitable for the calibrations, inspections, measurements and tests being carried out;

i) ensure that the handling, preservation and storage of inspection, measuring and test equipment is such that the accuracy and fitness for use is maintained;

j) safeguard inspection, measuring and test facilities including both test hardware and test software, from adjustments which would invalidate the calibration setting.

> *Where test hardware (e.g. jigs, fixtures, templates, patterns) or test software is used as suitable forms of inspection, they shall be checked to prove that they are capable of verifying the acceptability of product prior to release for use during production and installation and shall be rechecked at prescribed intervals. The supplier shall establish the extent and frequency of such checks and shall maintain records as evidence of control (see 4.16). Measurement design data shall be made available, when required by the purchaser or his representative, for verification that it is functionally adequate.*

- Establish and identify in the manual, procedures for the control, calibration and maintenance of all inspection, measuring and test equipment.
- Identify the measurements to be made, and the level of accuracy/precision required. Select appropriate inspection/measuring/test equipment that has the precision/accuracy required for the task. Ensure that the measurement uncertainty of the equipment is known and is consistent with the required measurement capability.
- Calibrate all equipment and devices at regular intervals or prior to use.
- The equipment must be calibrated against certified equipment having a known valid relationship to a recognized national/international standard. Where no standards exist, identify and document the basis used for calibration.
- Establish and maintain calibration procedures to include details of equipment type, identification number, location, frequency of checks, check method, acceptance criteria and action on nonconformances.
- Identify the calibration status by a suitable indicator or approved identification record.
- Maintain calibration records.
- If the equipment is found to be out of calibration, check to ensure the validity of preceding measurements taken by the same equipment.
- Establish adequate environmental conditions for calibration.
- Provide suitable storage facilities for the equipment to maintain a high degree of accuracy and fitness for use.
- Guard the equipment (software as well as hardware) against unauthorized tampering or adjustment.

- If test hard or test software is used for inspection, make sure that they are capable of verifying the product acceptability. Also, recheck such equipment at regular intervals.
- Establish and maintain a schedule and records of checks and rechecks of equipment to demonstrate evidence of control.
- Make available to the purchaser, when required, measurement design data for verification to ensure that it is functionally adequate.

4.12 INSPECTION AND TEST STATUS

The inspection and test status of product shall be identified by using markings, authorized stamps, tags, labels, routing cards, inspection records, test software, physical location or other suitable means, which indicate the conformance or non-conformance of product with regard to inspection and tests performed. The identification of inspection and test status shall be maintained, as necessary, throughout production and installation of the product to ensure that only product that has passed the required inspections and tests is despatched, used or installed.

Records shall identify the inspection authority responsible for the release of conforming product (see 4.16).

- Establish a system of identification of the product conformance/ nonconformance with regard to inspection/tests performed. The status can be identified using stamps, tags, markings, labels, routing cards, inspection records, test software, physical location, etc.
- Identify the inspection/test status throughout production cycle - from receipt to shipment.
- Designate and identify the inspection authority responsible for the release of conforming product.

4.13 CONTROL OF NONCONFORMING PRODUCT

The supplier shall establish and maintain procedures to ensure that product that does not conform to specified requirements is prevented from inadvertent use or installation. Control shall provide for identification, documentation, evaluation, segregation (when practical), disposition of nonconforming product and for notification to the functions concerned.

- Establish and list in the manual, all procedures regarding control of nonconforming product.
- Establish and maintain a system:
  - To ensure that nonconforming material is identified, documented and segregated, if possible.
  - To prevent the inadvertent use or installation of nonconforming material or product.
  - To evaluate the nature of nonconformity.
  - To notify the functions concerned.
  - To take appropriate action for the disposition of nonconforming material/product.

4.13.1 Nonconformity Review and Disposition

The responsibility for review and authority for the disposition of nonconforming product shall be defined.

Nonconforming product shall be reviewed in accordance with documented procedures. It may be

a) reworked to meet the specified requirements, or
b) accepted with or without repair by concession, or
c) re-graded for alternative applications, or
d) rejected or scrapped.

Where required by the contract, the proposed use or repair of product (see 4.13.1b) which does not conform to specified requirements shall be reported for concession to the purchaser or his representative. The description of nonconformity that has been accepted, and of repairs, shall be recorded to denote the actual condition (see 4.16).

Repaired and reworked product shall be re-inspected in accordance with documented procedures.

- Define, establish and identify the responsibility, authority, and procedures for review and disposition of nonconforming product.
- Possible modes of disposition can be:
  - Rework to meet specified requirements
  - Acceptance by concession
  - Re-grading for alternative use
  - Rejecting or scrapping
- If required by the contract, the proposed use or repair of the nonconforming product should be reported to the purchaser for concession. Also, the nature and description of nonconformity or repair, that has been mutually accepted by both parties, should be recorded to denote actual condition.
- Repaired/reworked product must be re-inspected.

4.14 CORRECTIVE ACTION

The supplier shall establish, document and maintain procedures for

a) investigating the cause of nonconforming product and the corrective action needed to prevent recurrence;

b) analyzing all processes, work operations, concessions, quality records, service reports and customer complaints to detect and eliminate potential causes of nonconforming product;

c) initiating preventative actions to deal with problems to a level corresponding to the risks encountered;

d) applying controls to ensure that corrective actions are taken and that they are effective;

e) implementing and recording changes in procedures resulting from corrective action.

- List in the manual, all corrective action procedures. Establish, document and maintain these procedures to:
  - Investigate causes of nonconformances.
  - Develop a corrective action plan to prevent recurrence.

- Analyze available information to identify and eliminate potential causes of nonconformances.
- Take corrective action to prevent recurrence.
- Monitor/audit/follow-up on corrective action implementation and its effectiveness.
- Maintain records of corrective action.
- Establish responsibility and authority for corrective action and how this action shall be carried out.

4.15 HANDLING, STORAGE, PACKAGING AND DELIVERY

4.15.1 General

The supplier shall establish, document and maintain procedures for handling, storage, packaging and delivery of product.

- Plan, develop and maintain documented procedures for handling, storage, packaging and delivery of incoming material, materials in process, and finished goods.

4.15.2 Handling

The supplier shall provide methods and means of handling that prevent damage or deterioration.

- Develop appropriate methods of handling materials to ensure prevention of damage or deterioration.

4.15.3 Storage

The supplier shall provide secure storage areas or stock rooms to prevent damage or deterioration of product, pending use or delivery. Appropriate methods for authorizing receipt and the despatch to and from such areas shall be stipulated. In order to detect deterioration, the condition of product in stock shall be assessed at appropriate intervals.

- Plan and secure suitable storage facilities, physical as well as environmental, to prevent deterioration of the product.
- Receipt and issue of material from stock areas must be controlled.
- Carry out periodical review of material in stock to detect deterioration.

4.15.4 Packaging

The supplier shall control packing, preservation and marking processes (including materials used) to the extent necessary to ensure conformance to specified requirements and shall identify, preserve and segregate all product from the time of receipt until the supplier's responsibility ceases.

- Control packaging procedures, materials and packaging designs to provide appropriate protection against damage or deterioration.
- Identify, preserve and segregate all product from the time of receipt until delivery.

4.15.5 Delivery

The supplier shall arrange for the protection of the quality of product after final inspection and test. Where contractually specified, this protection shall be extended to include delivery to destination.

- Provide suitable means of protecting the quality of product during all phases of delivery.

4.16 QUALITY RECORDS

The supplier shall establish and maintain procedures for identification, collection, indexing, filing, storage, maintenance and disposition of quality records.

Quality records shall be maintained to demonstrate achievement of the required quality and the effective operation of the quality system. Pertinent subcontractor quality records shall be an element of these data.

All quality records shall be legible and identifiable to the product involved. Quality records shall be stored and maintained in such a way that they are readily retrievable in facilities that provide a suitable environment to minimize deterioration or damage and to prevent loss. Retention times of quality records shall be established and recorded. Where agreed contractually, quality records shall be made available for evaluation by the purchaser or his representative for an agreed period.

- Develop and maintain a system to identify, select, index, file and store quality records.
- Quality records are used to demonstrate product quality and effective implementation of the quality system. Records to verify product quality include: quality plans; records of identification, traceability, inspection/test, and positive recall; records of nonconformance; document numbers; revision numbers. Records to verify effective system implementation include records pertaining to all the requisite system elements of ISO-9001.
- Quality records are to be legible and identifiable to the relevant product.
- Quality records are to be stored and maintained in such a way as to prevent deterioration and facilitate ease of retrieval.
- Establish, record, and implement procedures for retention times of the records.
- Arrangements should be established for making the records available to the purchaser or its representative for evaluation. Accordingly, relevant personnel should be notified of the agreed period for the storage of records.

4.17 INTERNAL QUALITY AUDITS

The supplier shall carry out a comprehensive system of planned and documented internal quality audits to verify whether quality activities comply with planned arrangements and to determine the effectiveness of the quality system.

Audits shall be scheduled on the basis of the status and importance of the activity.

The audits and follow-up actions shall be carried out in accordance with documented procedures.

The results of the audits shall be documented and brought to the attention of the personnel having responsibility in the area audited. The management personnel responsible for the area shall take timely corrective action on the deficiencies found by the audit (see 4.1.3).

- Establish and maintain a comprehensive system of planned and documented internal quality audits to verify effectiveness of the quality system activities.
- Establish appropriate audit schedules.
- Establish documented procedures for audits and follow-up actions.
- Audit findings must be documented and communicated to the responsible personnel as well as management for a timely corrective action.

4.18 TRAINING

The supplier shall establish and maintain procedures for identifying the training needs and provide for the training of all personnel performing activities affecting quality. Personnel performing specific assigned tasks shall be qualified on the basis of appropriate education, training and/or experience, as required. Appropriate records of training shall be maintained (see 4.16).

- Establish and maintain a system for identifying training needs.
- Provide training for all personnel whose activities effect quality and system implementation.
- For specific tasks, the assigned personnel must be qualified on the basis of appropriate education, training and experience.
- Maintain records of training activities.

4.19 SERVICING

Where servicing is specified in the contract, the supplier shall establish and maintain procedures for performing and verifying that servicing meets the specified requirements.

- If service function is part of the requirements, establish and maintain a procedure for performing and verifying that the service meets the specified requirements.
- Continuously check the quality of service provided.

4.20 STATISTICAL TECHNIQUES

Where appropriate, the supplier shall establish procedures for identifying adequate statistical techniques required for verifying the acceptability of process capability and product characteristics.

- Where appropriate, the use of statistical techniques is beneficial but not mandatory.
- Establish adequate statistical techniques to verify and monitor the acceptability of process performance/capability, or product characteristics.
- Statistical techniques include such methods as: sampling inspection plans, statistical process control, control charts, process capability analysis, design of experiments and other analytical problem solving techniques.

Note: 1. The text of the clauses 4.0 to 4.20 used in the above guidelines have been reproduced, without change, from ISO-9001. Permission to reproduce this text as well as the "Annex, ISO-9000 - 1987, page 6", reproduced in this book as "Table 20, page 105", has been granted by the Standards Council of Canada.

2. Copies of the ISO Standards can be obtained from the Standards Council of Canada (see page 111), who is the sole agent in Canada, for the sale of the ISO Standards.

FOURTEEN

QUALITY SYSTEM CHECKLIST

◆ INTRODUCTION

A checklist is a simple but extremely effective tool for ensuring propriety, validity and authenticity of a document, process or procedure. For ISO-9000 certification process, a checklist can be an invaluable tool to ensure adequate and accurate coverage of system elements and their effective implementation. Basically, the checklist can identify system strengths and weaknesses and assist in taking a prompt corrective action wherever appropriate to eliminate deficiencies.

◆ ISO-9000 CERTIFICATION: SYSTEM CHECKLIST

In so far as possible, a detailed checklist for the system elements of the chosen level of ISO-9000 standards should be prepared for use during the process of man-ual development and for the purpose of internal auditing. For the manual, the checklist can quickly identify if any system element has been either inadvertently missed or misrepresented. For the internal audit, the checklist makes the process of verification easier and ensures that all the systems are properly implemented and are functioning effectively and efficaciously. The checklist is an essential and invaluable tool for external audits also. Normally, the external auditors have a very exhaustive checklist against which they would audit the quality system of the organization for certification.

Unfortunately, there is no checklist yet available for the companies to use as an effective tool for auditing their own systems for ISO-9000 certification. In this chapter, we are including a checklist for the system elements of ISO-9001 developed from our own understanding and experience. We hope that this check-list will provide sufficient basic framework for manual development and internal auditing process. The users may modify this checklist and develop their own commensurate with their needs.

ISO-9001: QUALITY SYSTEM REQUIREMENTS: ACTION CHECKLIST

LEGEND

****	Adequate coverage
***	Improvement needed in system development/implementation
**	Fails to meet criteria in system development/implementation
*	Not applicable

SYSTEM ELEMENTS	****	***	**	*
4.1 MANAGEMENT RESPONSIBILITY				
4.1.1 Quality Policy				
• Quality policy defined/documented. • Quality objectives defined/documented. • Commitment to quality demonstrated. How? • Policy/objectives understood by all. How? • Policy/objectives implemented. How? • Policy/objectives maintained at all levels. How?				
4.1.2 Organization				
4.1.2.1 Responsibility and Authority				

• Quality responsibility/authority defined/
   documented.
• Responsible personnel designated/announced.
• Organizational chart established.
• Organizational structure developed to ensure its
   support for the achievement of quality goals.
• Designated personnel has freedom/authority to:
   • Take action to prevent nonconformity
   • Identify and record quality problems
   • Recommend/provide solutions				

SYSTEM ELEMENTS	* * * *	* * *	* *	*
• Verify implementation of solutions • Control/monitor further nonconformities.				
4.1.2.2 Verification Resources and Personnel				
• In-house verification requirements identified/ documented. • Adequate verification resources provided. • Trained personnel designated. • Verification/audit carried out by independent staff.				
4.1.2.3 Management Representative				
• Management representative appointed/authorized to ensure implementation/maintenance of quality system requirements. • Appointment announced and recorded in Quality Manual.				
4.1.3 Management Review				
• Senior management carries out review of quality system implementation/effectiveness at regular intervals. How? • Records of reviews maintained.				
4.2 QUALITY SYSTEM				
• Quality system established/maintained/documented as per ISO-9001. • Quality plans documented. • Quality Manual prepared/maintained. • Quality procedures/instructions documented. • Quality records/forms/books/files prepared and maintained. • Quality system being implemented as per Quality Manual.				

SYSTEM ELEMENTS	* * * *	* * * *	* *	*

4.3 CONTRACT REVIEW

- Contracts reviewed for adequacy of requirements. How?
- Discrepancies satisfactorily resolved. How?
- Contracts reviewed to ensure capability of meeting requirements. How?
- Contract review records maintained.
- Inter/intra communication maintained for contract review activities. How?

4.4 DESIGN CONTROL

4.4.1 General

- Control/verification procedures for all phases of design function developed/maintained. How?

4.4.2 Design and Development Planning

- Plans for design/development activity prepared/ documented/referenced.
- Design planning responsibility assigned.
- Design plans integrated with other relevant plans. How?
- Plans updated as design evolved. How?

4.4.2.1 Activity Assignment

- Qualified personnel assigned for design/ verification activities.
- Adequate resources provided to personnel. How?

4.4.2.2 Organizational and Technical Interfaces

- Organizational/technical interfaces established. How?

SYSTEM ELEMENTS	* * * *	* * *	* *	*
• Information documented/transmitted/reviewed regularly.				
4.4.3 Design Input				
• All pertinent design input requirements identified/ reviewed/recorded. How? • Ambiguities appropriately resolved. How?				
4.4.4 Design Output				
• Design output documented/expressed in terms of requirements. • Design output meets input requirements. • Design output contains reference acceptance criteria. How? • Design output meets appropriate regulatory requirements. How? • Design output identifies critical product safety factors. How?				
4.4.5 Design Verification				
• Design review/verification activities scheduled. • Competent personnel designated to verify design activities. • Design qualification tests/demonstrations carried out. How? • Design input/output capability and compatibility evaluated/verified. How? • New designs compared with similar proven designs.				
4.4.6 Design Changes				
• Procedures for design changes/modifications established. • Design changes reviewed/approved by appropriate persons. How?				

SYSTEM ELEMENTS	* * * * *	* * * *	* * *	*
4.5 DOCUMENT CONTROL				
4.5.1 Document Approval and Issue				
• Procedures established to control all quality system documents. How? • All documents pertaining to ISO-9001 system requirements reviewed/approved before issue. How? • Pertinent documents available at appropriate locations. • Obsolete documents promptly removed.				
4.5.2 Document Changes/Modifications				
• Changes to documents reviewed/approved by the same person who originally approved changes. • Designated persons have access to all requisite information upon which to base their review/ approval. How? • Changes identified in the document. How? • Control procedures established to prevent use of non-applicable documents. How? • Documents re-issued after several revisions.				
4.6 PURCHASING				
4.6.1 General				
• System/procedure established to ensure purchased product conforms to specified requirements. How?				
4.6.2 Assessment of Sub-contractors				
• Sub-contractors selected on the basis of their ability and performance record to meet requirements. How?				

SYSTEM ELEMENTS	* * * *	* * *	* *	*
• Records of acceptable sub-contractors kept. • Appropriate quality system controls maintained with the sub-contractors. How?				
4.6.3 Purchasing Data • Procurement data system established. How? • Purchasing documents clearly describe detailed information/data regarding ordered product. How? • Purchasing documents reviewed/approved for adequacy prior to release.				
4.6.4 Verification of Purchased Product • Purchaser afforded right to inspect/verify product at source or upon receipt. How?				
4.7 PURCHASER SUPPLIED PRODUCT • Procedures for verification/storage/maintenance of purchaser supplied product established/maintained. How? • Purchaser supplied product lost, damaged, or unsuitable for use recorded/reported to purchaser. How?				
4.8 PRODUCT IDENTIFICATION AND TRACEABILITY • Procedures established for identification/ traceability of product during all stages of production. How? • Identification is recorded. How?				

SYSTEM ELEMENTS	* * * *	* * *	* *	*

4.9 PROCESS CONTROL

4.9.1 General

- Production and installation operations performed under controlled conditions. How?
- Documented work instructions, process flow charts established for each process.
- All processes controlled through process control tools/methods, including SPC methods.

4.9.2 Special Processes

- Special processes employed are identified in the Quality Manual.
- Control conditions exercised for special processes. How?
- Special processes continuously monitored. How?
- Records of qualified processes/personnel/ equipment maintained. How?

4.10 INSPECTION AND TESTING

4.10.1 Receiving Inspection and Testing

- Quality plan/procedures for verifying incoming product established/documented. How?
- Procedures for handling nonconformities established. How?
- Procedures for product release, without incoming inspection, established. How?
- Procedures for positive recall established. How?

4.10.2 In-Process Inspection and Testing

- Quality plan/procedures for in-process inspection/ testing established. How?

SYSTEM ELEMENTS	* * * *	* * *	* *	*
• Process control methods used to control/monitor quality. How? • Product hold, release, or positive recall procedures established. How? • Procedures for handling nonconformities established. How?				
4.10.3 Final Inspection and Testing • Quality plan/procedures for final inspection established. How? • Quality plan indicates that requisite inspection/ testing carried out on receipt of product or in-process and data meets specified requirements. • Product not shipped unless inspection results indicate conformance. • Conformance results data/documentation available and authorized. How? **4.10.4 Inspection and Test Records** • Inspection/test records maintained to verify conformance. How? • Acceptance criteria defined/documented. How?				
4.11 INSPECTION, MEASURING AND TEST EQUIPMENT • Calibration procedures established/documented/ maintained for all inspection, measuring and test equipment. How? • Measuring/test equipment selected/tested as per accuracy/precision required. How? • Measuring/test equipment calibrated against certified national/international standards. How? • Calibration status of equipment identified by a suitable indicator. How? • Calibration status/records maintained. How?				

SYSTEM ELEMENTS	* * * * *	* * * *	* *	*
• When equipment found to be out of calibration, the validity of results of previous inspections assessed/ documented. How? • Suitable environmental conditions/storage/ equipment established for calibration/inspections/ tests carried out. How? • Procedures established to guard against unauthorized tampering/adjustment. How? • Calibration procedures for test hardware/software established. How?				
4.12 INSPECTION AND TEST STATUS • Procedures established for identifying inspection/test status of product. How? • Status of product conformance/non-conformance with regard to inspection/tests maintained throughout production cycle. How? • Record of personnel authorized for release of conforming product maintained. How?				
4.13 CONTROL OF NONCONFORMING PRODUCT • Control procedures established to handle non-conforming material/product. • Nonconforming material identified/documented/ segregated (if possible). How? • Nonconforming material prevented from use. How? • Nonconformities reported to functions concerned. How?				

SYSTEM ELEMENTS	* * * *	* * *	* *	*
4.13.1 Nonconformity Review and Disposition				
• Personnel identified/authorized for disposition of nonconforming material. How? • Procedures established/documented for review and disposition of nonconforming product. How? • Action required on nonconforming product identified and reported to the purchaser. How? • Description of nonconformity recorded. How? • Repaired/reworked product reinspected in accordance with documented procedures. How?				
4.14 CORRECTIVE ACTION				

• Procedures established/documented/maintained for:
  • Investigating cause of nonconforming product. How?
  • Corrective action to prevent recurrence of nonconformities. How?
  • Analysis to detect/eliminate potential causes of nonconforming product. How?
  • Ensuring that corrective action has been taken. How?
  • Assessing to identify the effectiveness of the corrective action. How?
  • Implementing/recording changes in procedures resulting from corrective action. How?				

4.15 HANDLING, STORAGE, PACKAGING AND DELIVERY **4.15.1 General** • Procedures established for handling/storage/ packaging/delivery of all material. How?				

SYSTEM ELEMENTS	* * * *	* * * *	* * *	*
4.15.2 Handling				
• Proper procedures established for handling material to prevent damage/deterioration. How?				
4.15.3 Storage				
• Suitable storage facilities established. How? • Control procedures established for receipt/issue of material from stock. How? • Periodical review of material in stock carried out to detect deterioration. How?				
4.15.4 Packaging				
• Control procedures established for packing, preservation, marking process, packaging design to ensure conformance to specified requirements. How? • Packaging procedures established so as to prevent damage/deterioration for the entire cycle of production to delivery. How?				
4.15.5 Delivery				
• Procedures established for protection of product after final inspection/test. How? • Product quality protection provided during all phases of delivery. How?				
4.16 QUALITY RECORDS				
• Procedures established/maintained for identification, collection, indexing, filing, storage, maintenance, disposition of quality records. How? • Quality records, including procurement records of subcontractors, utilized to demonstrate effective functioning of the quality system. How?				

SYSTEM ELEMENTS	*⁣*⁣*⁣*	*⁣*⁣*	*⁣*	*
• Quality records clearly identifiable to product involved. How? • Quality records stored/maintained effectively to prevent deterioration/damage/loss. How? • Quality records readily retrievable. How? • Procedure established to make quality records available to purchaser for evaluation. How?				
4.17 INTERNAL QUALITY AUDITS • Comprehensive internal quality audit system established to verify effectiveness of quality system activities. How? • Audit schedule developed in relation to status/ importance of activity. How? • Audits/follow-up actions carried out in accordance with documented procedures. How? • Audit results documented/reported to responsible personnel and management for timely corrective action. How?				
4.18 TRAINING • Training needs identified. • Appropriate training provided. How? • Personnel assigned to specific tasks are qualified on the basis of education/training/experience. How? • Records of training activities kept. How?				

SYSTEM ELEMENTS	* * * *	* * *	* *	*
4.19 SERVICING • Procedures for providing effective service established/maintained. How? • Service quality effectiveness continuously verified. How?				
4.20 STATISTICAL TECHNIQUES • Where appropriate, statistical techniques used to analyze/improve operations. How?				

BIBLIOGRAPHY

●

REFERENCES

A. BIBLIOGRAPHY

1. Ackerman, R.B. et al (1987): "Process Quality Management and Improvement Guidelines". AT&T Bell Laboratories, P.O. Box 19901, Indianapolis, Indiana.

2. Canadian Standards Association: National Standard of Canada: "CAN-Q395-81: Quality Audits". Canadian Standards Association, Rexdale, Ontario, Canada.

3. Crosby, P.B. (1979): "Quality is Free.": McGraw-Hill Book Company, New York, U.S.A.

4. Deming, W. E. (1982): "Out of the Crisis": Massachusetts Institute of Technology, Massachussets, U.S.A.

5. Dzus, George (1991): "Planning a Successful ISO-9000 Assessment": Quality Progress - American Society for Quality Control, November 1991, pp. 43-46.

6. International Organization for Standardization (ISO), Central Secretariate, Geneva.

   - ISO-8402 (1986): Quality Vocabulary
   - ISO/CD 8402-1: Quality Concepts and Terminology, Part 1: Generic Terms and Definitions. Under preparation.
   - ISO-2382/1: Data Processing - Vocabulary, Part 1: Fundamental Terms.
   - ISO-9000: Quality Management and Quality Assurance Standards:
     - Part 2: Guide for the Implementation of ISO-9001, ISO-9002, ISO-9003. Under preparation.
     - Part 3 (1991): Guidelines for the Application of ISO-9001 to the Development, Supply and Maintenance of Software.
   - ISO/DIS 9004-2 (1991): Quality Management and Quality System Elements - Part 2: Guidelines for Services.
   - Quality Management: Guidelines for Developing Quality Manuals. Under preparation.

- ISO-10011: Guidelines for Auditing Quality Systems:
  - Part 1 (1990): Auditing
  - Part 2 (1991): Qualifications Criteria for Quality System Auditors
  - Part 3 (1991): Management of Audit Programs

7. Juran, J.M. (1986): "The Quality Trilogy": Quality Progress - American Society for Quality Control, August 1986, pp. 19-24.

8. Juran, J.M. (1989): "Leadership for Quality": Free Press, New York.

9. Lamprecht, J.L. (1991): "ISO-9000 Implementation Strategies" - Quality. November 1991, pp. 14-17.

10. Lofgren, G.Q. (1991): "Quality System Registration": Quality Progress - American Society for Quality Control, May 1991, pp. 35-37.

11. Mills, C.A. (1989): "The Quality Audit: A Management Evaluation Tool,": ASQC Quality Process, Milwaukee and McGraw-Hill Book Co., New York.

12. Miuro, Akio (1989): "Don't Suffer Through Bad Manuals": Quality Progress - American Society for Quality Control, December 1989, pp. 96.

13. Mizuno, Shigeru (1988): "Management for Quality Improvement - The Seven New QC Tools". Productivity Press, Cambridge, Massachussetts.

14. Rosander, A.C. (1991): "Deming's 14 Points Applied to Services". Marcel Dekker, Inc., New York and ASQC Quality Press, Milwaukee, Wisconsin.

B. AUTHOR'S REFERENCES

A large part of the material presented in this book has been extracted from the author's teaching and consulting notes, published books and professional papers. A selected list of references is as follows:

PUBLISHED BOOKS

1. Puri, S.C. (1989): "Statistical Methods for Food Quality Management". Publication number A73-5268. Agriculture Canada, Ottawa, Canada.

2. Puri, S.C. (1984): "Statistical Process Quality Control - Key to Productivity". Standards-Quality Management Group, Ottawa, Canada.

3. Puri, S.C. (1981): "Statistical Aspects of Food Quality Assurance." Publication Number 5140. Agriculture Canada, Ottawa, Canada.

4. Puri, S.C. and Mullen, K. (1980): "Applied Statistics for Food and Agricultural Scientists". G.K. Hall & Co., Boston, Massachussets.

5. Puri, S.C., Ennis, D. and Mullen, K. (1979): "Statistical Quality Control for Food and Agricultural Scientists". G.K. Hall & Co., Boston, Massachusetts.

TECHNICAL PAPERS

1. Puri, S.C. (1992): "The ABC's of Implementing ISO-9000": Transactions, 46th Annual Quality Congress -American Society for Quality Control, Nashville, Tennessee.

2. Puri, S.C. (1991): "Deming and ISO-9000: A Deadly Combination for Quality Revolution": Transactions, 45th Annual Quality Congress - American Society for Quality Control, Milwaukee, Wisconsin.

3. Puri, S.C. (1990): "Food Safety and Quality Control: SPC with HACCP": Transactions, 44th Annual Quality Congress - American Society for Quality Control, San Fransico, California.

4. Puri, S.C. (1989): "Genesis of Statistical Process Control": Transactions, Update 89 Seminar. The Institute of Environmental Science and the Society of Reliability Engineers, Ottawa, Canada.

5. Puri, S.C. (1989): "Continuous Improvement: Master Check-list": Transaction, 43rd Annual Quality Congress - American Society for Quality Control, Toronto, Canada.

6. Puri, S.C. (1988): "Applied SPC and the Taguchi Approach": Transactions, 19th International Symposium on Applied Technology and Automation, Monte Carlo, Monaco.

7. Puri, S.C. (1988): "International Perspectives on Quality and Standardization": Transactions, 34th Annual Quality Forum - American Society for Quality Control, Toronto Section, Toronto, Canada.

8. Puri, S.C. (1987): "Agri-Food Business: The Years Ahead": Transactions, 2nd Seminar of the European Organization for Quality Control - Section for QC in the Food Industry, Zurich, Switzerland.

9. Puri, S.C. (1987): "Developing Countries - A National Plan for Quality-Productivity": Transactions, International Conference - International Association of Science and Technology for Development, Paris, France.

10. Puri, S.C. (1987): "Management of Food Quality: Issues and Trends": Transactions, 33rd Annual Quality Forum - American Society for Quality Control, Toronto Section, Toronto, Canada.

11. Puri, S.C. (1987): "Quality Challenges and Opportunities for Developing Countries": Transactions, 31st Annual Conference - European Organization for Quality Control, Munich, W. Germany.

12. Puri, S.C. (1987): "A Plan of Excellence for a Regulatory Agency": Transactions, 41st Annual Quality Congress - American Society for Quality Control, Minneapolis, Minnesota.

13. Puri, S.C. (1987): "Estimation of Weibull Distribution Parameters for Failure Analysis": Transactions, International Conference - International Association of Science and Technology for Development, Los Angeles, California.

14. Puri, S.C. (1986): "A Master Plan for Quality-Productivity": Transactions, 7th Latin American Quality Control Congress, Saltillo, Mexico.

15. Puri, S.C. (1985): "Quality and Deregulation": Transactions, 40th Annual Quality Congress - American Society for Quality Control, Anaheim, California.

16. Puri, S.C. (1984): "Quality Registration Programs": Transactions, World Quality Congress - European Organization for Quality Control, Brighton, U.K.

17. Puri, S.C. (1983): "Quality, Standardization and Developing Countries": Transactions, II-Asia Pacific Congress, Mexico City, Mexico.

18. Puri, S.C. (1983): "Quality Indicators for Corporate Management": Transactions, 37th Annual Quality Congress - American Society for Quality Control, Boston, Massachusetts.

19. Puri, S.C. (1983): "Quality Management and Cost-Recovery": Transactions, 37th Annual Quality Congress - American Society for Quality Control, Boston, Massachusetts.

20. Puri, S.C. and McWhinnie, J. (1981): "Quality Management Through Quality Indicators - A New Approach": Quality Assurance - Methods, Management and Motivation. Society of Manufacturing Engineers and American Society for Quality Control, U.S.A.

21. Puri, S.C. (1980): "The Role of Standardization in the Manufacturing of Products, Goods, Exchange, and Services": Transactions, 24th European Organization for Quality Control, Warsaw, Poland.

22. Puri, S.C. (1979): "Management of Total Reliability": Microelectronics and Reliability, Vol. 19, No. 1/2, pp. 7-10.

23. Puri, S.C. (1978): "Quality Control and Reliability": Engineering and Statistical Research Institute, Agriculture Canada, Ottawa, Report q-58, pp. 6-7.

24.   Puri, S.C. (1976): "Application of MINQUE Procedures to Block Designs": Communications in Statistics. Vol. 5, No. 2, pp. 191-196.

25.   Puri, S.C. (1974): "Panel Grading of Butter - a Feasibility Study": Proceedings XIX International Dairy Congress, New Delhi, India.

INDEX

The Author

Subhash C. Puri is the Director of Quality Assurance and Statistics at Agriculture Canada. As Chief Statistician, he is responsible for providing advice and direction to corporate management on all matters relating to quality management, standardization, and statistical applications. As one of the leading experts in the field of quality, he has taught and lectured, for over two decades, at various organizations and institutions in several countries, and has provided extensive training and consultation to numerous companies in the manufacturing and service sectors.

He is very actively involved in the national and international standardization activities. He is the Chairman of CAC/ISO/TC 69, member of CAC/ISO/TC 176 and has served as chairman/member on many other standards committees. He is the author of several books and has published numerous professional papers on the subject. He provides several training courses in quality management at the Professional Development Centre of Carleton University.